D0401417

CONTENTS

atheist — *n.* One who denies the existence of God [MF < Gk. *a-*, without + *theos*, God]

GOD
DOESN'T BELIEVE
in
ATHEISTS

Proof that the atheist

doesn't exist

RAY COMFORT

Bridge-Logos *Publishers*

Gainesville, Florida 32614 USA

Bridge-Logos

Orlando, FL 32822 USA

Printed in the United States of America.

Library of Congress Catalog Card Number: 93-072222
International Standard Book Number 0-88270-922-4

Unless otherwise indicated, Scripture quotations are from the *New King James Version*, © 1979, 1980, 1982 by Thomas Nelson Inc., Publishers, Nashville, Tennessee.

Scripture quotations designated KJV are from the *King James Version*.

G163.319x.S.m608.35250

FOREWORD

A RUSSIAN SCIENTIST visiting an American university said, "Either there is a God or there isn't. Both possibilities are frightening!" This is so true. If there is a God, we need to find out who He is and what He wants. If there is no God, we are in trouble. We are hurtling through space at 66,000 mph and no one is in charge. What a frightening thought!

In this book Ray Comfort does an excellent job of showing how illogical the atheist's position is. Why would anyone with eyes to see and a mind to think claim to be an atheist? Isn't it obvious that design demands a designer? If you were walking through the woods and found a painting hanging on a tree, you would automatically conclude that it did not grow out of the tree. Even though the painting is made of all natural components, it is quite apparent from all human experience that these things don't happen without intelligent input. Even if you never see the painter, it is obvious there is one somewhere.

How did this amazing world get here? In my 33 years of studying the topic of creation vs. evolution, I have never met an atheist who did not believe in evolution to justify his worldview. Yet, in the 140 years since Darwin made the evolution theory popular, not one shred of real scientific evidence has been found to show how this complex universe could have come into its present form without an intelligent Designer. Just as one must have faith in evolution, one must also have faith that there is no God. Both evolution and atheism are religions.

Ray Comfort's goal in this book is to bring the atheist face to face with the facts and make him realize that the very God he claims not to believe in loves him anyway and wants to forgive his sin. It is my hope and prayer that this book will help every open-minded atheist come to know the Creator of the universe as his personal Savior.

DR. KENT HOVIND
Creation Science Evangelism
Pensacola, Florida (www.drdino.com)

INTRODUCTION

I ONCE WROTE to the American Atheists, Inc., and offered to speak at their national convention. I told them that I had the necessary credentials to do so, having spoken at Yale University on the subject of atheism and published a booklet called "The Atheist Test," which had sold hundreds of thousands of copies. I concluded the letter by saying that I had also written a book on the subject: *God Doesn't Believe in Atheists*. They promptly turned me down.

I was flattered that they didn't want me to speak, but at the same time I was a little disappointed. I had prayed that they would—after all, the Bible does say, "With God, nothing will be impossible" (Luke 1:37). I guess I was a little naive. The thought of hundreds of atheists actually allowing a preacher to address them at a national convention is ridiculous.

Some time later I found myself crossing swords with Ron Barrier (the spokesperson for American Atheists, Inc.) via email. At one point he challenged me to a debate. He then read the book you are holding and quickly withdrew the offer.

Shortly after that incident, a number of other atheists began writing to me and when one called me a "chicken," I told him that Ron Barrier had "chickened out" of a debate. They roasted him to a point where he admitted to it, renewed the offer, and then "sweetened the pot" by flying me from Los Angeles to Florida to debate at their 2001 national convention. I was delighted.

It was a wonderful experience.[1] Ron Barrier and I co-signed my book together for their library, and we even hugged after the debate. With God, *nothing* will be impossible.

Chapter One

WHO MADE GOD?

S OMEONE WITH dry wit once made me laugh when he mumbled, "Come in, boat number nine. Please come in, boat number nine. Boat number nine, can you hear me? Wait a minute—we don't have a boat number nine! Boat number six—*are you in trouble?*"

It amazes me that people can have a belief in the existence of God, and yet not think for a minute that something is radically wrong in our world. They can smile while boat number six sits upside-down in the water, slowly sinking.

Let's look at an average day on God's fair earth. The day dawns to find that (according to UNICEF) 20,000 children have starved to death during the night. Another 20,000 children and many thousands of adults will die today of severe malnutrition. Nothing new there. Thousands of people will die after being bitten by poisonous snakes, spiders, or scorpions; attacked by sharks (84 unprovoked attacks worldwide in 2001); devoured by lions, tigers, and other man-eating killers; or infected with diseases from blood-sucking mosquitoes.

Perhaps today we will have a surprise volcanic eruption, or an earthquake that will crush families to death beneath the debris of their homes. Cancerous diseases will continue to take their toll and cause thousands to die in agony. Multitudes will perish from fatal ailments that have always plagued mankind, from asthma to typhoid to leprosy to heart disease. Today, human beings will be struck by lightning, drowned in floods, stung to death by killer bees, killed by hurricanes and tornadoes, and tormented by blight, pestilence, and infestations. They will be afflicted, devastated, and brought to ruin.

The fact is, there are only three alternatives to explain all this suffering:

1. There is no God, as evidenced by the chaos.

2. God is totally incompetent and can't control His creation (or won't, which makes Him a tyrant).

3. There is another explanation, one which the Bible gives for the state of the world.

Let's take a rational, logical look at the first of these three possibilities. It is the basis of a philosophy commonly called "atheism."

Faith Is for Wimps

From my own experience and from listening to many objections to Christianity, I have found that the subject of faith is often offensive to the nonbeliever. My own thinking was that faith was for the weak-minded, for little old ladies, and for those near death. Yet every belief we have about history, other countries, science, biology, etc., exists because of faith. You only believe as you do because you believed the person who told you the information. You don't *know* who discovered America. You simply have faith that what was told to you is indeed true. Neither do you *know* if General Custer died at the hands of Indians, or if Napoleon really existed.

We can't live without faith. Try it. Say to yourself, "Today, I refuse to exercise any faith at all." Then before you eat your corn flakes, go through every flake, scientifically testing it before you eat it. Refuse to trust that the manufacturers have obeyed health regulations and mixed the ingredients correctly. Do the same tests on the milk before you pour it on the corn flakes, in faith. You don't know that the milk processors have done their job and given you pure milk. They may have mixed in something that could be harmful to your health.

Don't trust the sugar producers either. God only knows what they did while they were processing the sugar. Then check the microscope and other tools used for your analysis. How can you really trust that the information you gather from them is reliable? Don't trust your weight to the chair at the breakfast table. Don't believe today's weather report or any news item until you actually go to the proper location and see for yourself if what they would have you believe is true. Even then you will have to trust your natural senses (which can't always be trusted).

WE EITHER LIVE WITH FAITH OR FALL VICTIM TO PARANOIA.

Before you drink your coffee, don't trust that the cup is perfectly clean. Wash it out yourself. Don't use untested water, in faith. We really don't know what's in it nowadays; it may be contaminated. And be sure to analyze the coffee. If you decide to take a taxi to work, you will have to trust your life to the vehicle and the taxi driver, and trust the other drivers to stay on their side of the road. You will have to trust elevators, stairways, airplanes, the post office, and banks. Believe me—we either live with faith or fall victim to paranoia.

If, then, faith so evidently surrounds us, why should it be so offensive? It is simply because faith is as essential to the spiritual realm as oxygen is to the natural realm. The professing atheist thinks that if he can get rid of any thought of faith, he can get rid of Christianity. In trying to do so, he saws through the branch he is sitting on. His own faith in the erroneous information he has makes him think he is atheistic in his beliefs.

Trump Card

I have found from experience that the popular atheist's question, "Who made God?" doesn't deserve to have a question mark. It is usually presented as a statement. The questioner is persuaded that such a question cannot be answered. A twinkle is usually seen in his eye as he tosses onto the table what he thinks is his trump card. He gambles his very soul on the belief that there is no higher card—that the question *cannot* be answered.

Actually, the explanation is very simple. For the answer, all I need is to be able to reason with you, and for you to be *reasonable*.

Does space have an end? If it does—if there is a brick wall at the end of space that reads "The End"—I want to know what's behind the brick wall. By faith we are forced to believe that no matter in which direction we set off, space will never end. It just goes on and on and on—forever. It has no beginning or end. It stresses the brain to think about such a state, but we have no choice but to accept that fact by faith.

God also has no beginning and no end. But with God, we have a little more information than we have with space. Time is a dimension that God has created and it is to this dimension that mankind is subjected. We have to wait for time to pass. We can't jump ahead even one second in time. We are enslaved in its power. It is because we are in time that reason demands a beginning and an end. It stresses the brain to think of any other dimension.

However, God is not subject to the dimension of time. He dwells in eternity. The Bible tells us that to God a day is the same as a thousand years (see 2 Peter 3:8). You can prove this for yourself by studying the prophecies of the Bible mentioned in a later chapter. God can flick through time as you and I flick through the pages of a history book. If you find this hard to believe, even when confronted with the evidence of biblical prophecies, you will find it to be true one day. The Scriptures tell us that God will eventually withdraw time, and we will then dwell in eternity.

The Christian is told that he *understands* "by faith." For instance, if I have major surgery, I trust the surgeon even though I have no real understanding of how he is going to operate. I have to trust him or there will be no operation. I understand that he has the ability to make me well, so I have faith in him.

In the same manner, I trust God. Many have died at the hands of surgeons, but no one perishes in the hands of God. His ability is boundless and His promises are "an anchor of the soul, both sure and steadfast" (Hebrews 6:19). Doctors[2] and pilots will fail you, friends you trust will disappoint you, elevators will let you down, but the promises of Almighty God are utterly trustworthy. This may be hard for you to appreciate at this time, but I want to encourage you to have an open mind as we look closely at the subject of atheism.

The Atheist Test

I don't believe in atheists. This isn't because I haven't met people who claim the title, but because such a person cannot exist.

Let's imagine that you are a professing atheist. I will ask you two questions:

First, do you know the combined weight of all the sand on all the beaches of Hawaii? I think I can safely assume that you don't. This brings us to the second question: Do you know how many hairs are on the back of a fully grown male Tibetan yak? Probably not. Therefore, it is reasonable for me to conclude that there are some things you don't know. It is important to ask these questions because there are some people who think they know everything.

Let's say that you know an incredible one percent of all the knowledge in the universe. To know 100 percent, you would have to know absolutely everything. There wouldn't be a rock in the universe that you would not be intimately familiar with, or a grain of sand that you would not be aware of. You would know everything that has happened in history, from that which is common knowledge to the minor details of the secret love life of Napoleon's great-grandmother's black cat's fleas. You would know every hair of every head, and every thought of every heart. All history would be laid out before you, because you would be omniscient (all-knowing).

> THE "ATHEIST" CAN'T FIND GOD FOR THE SAME REASON A THIEF CAN'T FIND A POLICEMAN.

Bear in mind that one of the greatest scientists who ever lived, Thomas Edison, said, "We do not know a millionth of one percent about anything." Let me repeat: Let's say that you have an incredible *one percent* of all the knowledge in the universe. Would it be possible, in the ninety-nine percent of the knowledge that you haven't yet come across, that there might be ample evidence to prove the existence of God? If you are reasonable, you will be forced to admit that it is possible. Somewhere, in the vast knowledge you haven't yet discovered, there could be enough evidence to prove that God does exist.

Let's look at the same thought from another angle. If I

were to make an absolute statement such as, "There is no gold in China," what is needed for that statement to be proven true? I need absolute or total knowledge. I need to know that there is no gold in any rock, in any river, in the ground, in any store, in any ring, or in any filling in any mouth in China. If there is one speck of gold in China, then my statement is false and I have no basis for it. I need absolute knowledge before I can make an absolute statement. Conversely, for me to say, "There *is* gold in China," does not require that I have all knowledge. I just need to have seen a speck of gold in the country, and the statement is then true.

To say categorically, "There is no God," is to make an absolute statement. For the statement to be true, I must know for certain that there is no God in the entire universe. No human being has all knowledge. Therefore, none of us is able to truthfully make this assertion.

If you insist upon disbelief in God, what you must say is, "Having the limited knowledge I have at present, I *believe* that there is no God." Owing to a lack of knowledge on your part, you don't *know* if God exists. So, in the strict sense of the word, you cannot be an atheist. The only true qualifier for the title is the One who has absolute knowledge, and why on earth would God want to deny His own existence?

The professing atheist is what is commonly known as an "agnostic"—one who claims to not know if God exists, or "one who professes ignorance." The Bible tells us that this ignorance is willful: "The wicked in his proud countenance does not seek God; God is in none of his thoughts" (Psalm 10:4). It's not that a person *can't* find God, but that he *won't*. It has been rightly said that the "atheist" can't find God for the same reason a thief can't find a policeman. He knows that if he admits there is a God, he is admitting that he is ultimately responsible to Him. This is not a pleasant thought for some.

It is said that Mussolini (the Italian dictator) once stood on a pinnacle and cried, "God, if you are there, strike me dead!" When God didn't immediately bow to his dictates, Mussolini then concluded that there was no God. However, his prayer *was* answered some time later.

Chapter Two

BANANA IN HAND

I S IT POSSIBLE to prove that God does exist? To begin to answer this, let me share with you an intellectually stimulating theory. It is my theory of where the Coca-Cola® can may have come from:

Billions of years ago, an incredibly big bang occurred. It came from nothing and from nowhere, sending a massive rock spinning through space (which also appeared from nowhere). As the rock cooled, a brown, sweet bubbly liquid formed on its surface.

As time passed, aluminum crept out of the liquid and formed itself into a can, made a lid, then a tab on the top of the lid.

Millions of years later, red and white paint fell from the sky and clung to the can, forming itself into the words, "Coca-Cola Classic®, Original Formula, 12 FL OZ."

You may feel intellectually insulted by such thoughts. So you should. Such irrationalism is beneath your academic dignity. You know that if the Coca-Cola can has a design, there *must* be a designer. If it is *made*, there *must* be a maker. The alternative—that it happened by accident—is unreasonable, illogical, and absurd to say the least.

Now, to help me bring what I am saying to a point, I would appreciate it if you would be kind enough to go find a banana. It will be well worth your time and effort.

Exhibit A

I presume you have the banana in hand (if not in hand, in mind). We will call it "Exhibit A." If you have found a well-made banana, you will notice that the far side has three ridges, and the near side has two ridges.[3] Notice how neatly it fits into the human hand. Feel how it has been made with a non-slip surface. It also has outward indicators of the inward contents: green—too early; yellow—just right; black—too late.

Now take a look at the top and see how (like the Coca-Cola can) it has been made with a "tab" so that it can be simply opened. Note that when you pull the tab the contents don't squirt in your face. Also note that there are perforations on the wrapper (usually four) so that it will sit gracefully over the human hand.

The wrapper is environmentally sound. It is made of a biodegradable substance that will in time decompose into banana-growing soil.

Notice how the banana is the right size for the human mouth. There is a point at the top for ease of entry. Now put it into your mouth and give your taste buds a treat. Not only will they be delighted, but so will your whole body. The banana is full of body-building nutrients and is easy for the stomach to digest. What's more, the Maker of the banana has even curved it toward the face to make the whole process so much easier.

Exhibit B

Now, if you would be so kind, put the banana down and get an apple (this won't make any sense if you don't). Take the apple in your right hand and study its form. Notice how it's perfectly shaped for the human hand. Its several thousand varieties are similarly shaped. On one end it has a large groove, made for the human thumb. On the other end is a smaller groove, made for the human forefinger. The thumb-groove has a stem that is flexible, so that it won't go up under the thumbnail. The smaller groove has a "pad" so that when the apple turns, it doesn't wear out the finger.

The apple has an advantage over the banana in that you may eat its wrapper. On the inside you will find a chewy, palatable substance that is pleasant to the taste buds and beneficial for the body. When you get to the core of the substance, you will find something most of us take for granted. So that you won't be disheartened when the apple is gone, the Manufacturer has (completely free of charge) placed small black seeds in the middle. When these are placed into the soil, they form trees that produce more apples.

THE WHOLE OF CREATION DRIPS WITH GOD'S GOODNESS TO HUMANITY.

The whole of creation drips with God's goodness to humanity. The next time you hold a nice big chunk of watermelon on a hot summer day, think about how kind your Creator is to give you a cool, sweet liquid in a watertight container. What's more, the container itself can be cut into slices and the flesh of the fruit consumed. Succulent grapes hang in a bunch waiting to be plucked by the human hand and dropped into the open mouth. Pistachio nuts split their sides to let us know that they are ready and willing to be eaten. The walnut sits in its protective case, like a tiny human brain, until it is cracked open by a nut lover. Sweet peas line up in their pod in order of size, awaiting a hand to squeeze the pliable wrapper. Apricots drip with a luscious liquid that makes the mouth water at the mere thought. Peaches, like the cheeks of a baby, blush on the tree to let the grower know that they are ready to be consumed. Heat from the sun transforms the lemon from green to yellow to let us know it is ready for those with a taste for tart. Oranges pile high in the supermarket stack, as hand-sized leak-free containers of a sweet, healthy liquid. Even when the wrapper is peeled away, each of the removable edible segments of juice is self-sealed and mouth-shaped.

Albert Einstein was right when he said that we either see nothing in life as a miracle, or everything as a miracle. The professing atheist has a far, far greater chance of convincing me that no one designed the Coca-Cola can than he has of persuading me that all created things have no Creator. Just as it's an insult to the intellect to say that paint "formed itself" into words on a can, it is infinitely more absurd to even momentarily entertain the smallest thought that everything made has no Maker.

What chance would I have of convincing you that this book had no author, no printer, and no publisher? Everything came from nothing. Ink just appeared, formed itself into legible words which formed coherent sentences, which fell into place on the paper, which came into being from nothing. Numbers on each page fell into order by mere chance. The pages then bound and trimmed themselves into the paperback size. Could I convince you that the design on the cover had no designer?

A Matter of Faith

I once heard a well-known preacher say, "You can't prove God or disprove Him. It's all a matter of faith." I disagree. The existence of God has nothing to do with "faith." Let me tell you why.

When I look at a building, how do I know that there was a builder? I can't see him, hear him, touch, taste, or smell him. Of course, the building is proof that there was a builder. In fact, I couldn't want better evidence that there was a builder than to have the building in front of me. I don't need "faith" to know that there was a builder. All I need is eyes that can see and a brain that works.

This same profound, intellectual principle applies to paintings and painters. When I look at a painting, how can I know that there was a painter? Why, the painting is perfectly positive proof that there was a painter. In fact, I couldn't want better scientific evidence that there was a painter than to have the painting in front of me. Isn't it true? I don't need "faith" to believe in a painter. All I need is eyes that can see and a brain that works. This is so simple that a child can understand it. The only ones who have trouble with its simplicity are those who profess to be intellectuals. No wonder someone once said that the certain proof that intelligent life exists elsewhere in the universe is that no one has bothered to make contact with us. However, I am pleased to say that I have seen professing atheists suddenly backslide from their beliefs when they have paused for a moment and thought about it. It's as though a light goes on in their mind. Take for instance this posting from the American Atheists, Inc. online message board:

> I recently watched a videotape loaned to me by a Christian friend. It was a recording of Ron Barrier's debate with a New Zealander concerning the existence of a god, recorded from AA's convention this past spring. I was intrigued by the debate and a little shaken—the [New Zealander's] argument for design was compelling.

The same principle of building/builder, painting/painter applies with the existence of God. Nothing on this earth that was "made" has no maker. When I look at creation, how can I know that there was a Creator? I can't see Him, hear Him, touch Him, taste Him, or smell Him. How can I know that He exists? Why, creation proves, beyond the shadow of the smallest doubt, that there is a Creator. You *cannot* have a "creation" without a Creator (Webster's dictionary defines "creation" as "the act of creating; especially the act of bringing the world into ordered existence"). I couldn't want better scientific proof that a Creator exists than to have creation in front of me. I don't need "faith" to believe in a Creator—all I need is eyes that can see and a brain that works.

> For since the creation of the world His invisible attributes are clearly seen [by the eyes that can see], being understood [by a brain that works] by the things that are made, even His eternal power and Godhead, so that they are without excuse (Romans 1:20).

If, however, I want the builder to do something for me, *then* I need to have faith in him. This is where faith enters, in the form of trust:

> Without faith it is impossible to please Him, for he who comes to God must believe that He is, and that He is a rewarder of those who diligently seek Him (Hebrews 11:6).

Let me put it another way: He who comes to God must not believe that He doesn't exist, for only without doubt is it possible to please Him.

What About Science?

Professing atheists often point to science as if it provided evidence for *their* cause. For example, Madalyn Murray O'Hair,[4] the founding president of American Atheists, Inc., once said:

> The indestructible foundation of the whole edifice of Atheism is its philosophy—materialism, or naturalism,

as it is also known. That philosophy regards the world as it actually is, views it in the light of the data provided by progressive science and social experience. Atheistic materialism is the logical outcome of scientific knowledge gained over the centuries.

However, did you know that the word "science" means "knowledge"? The building/builder reasoning is scientific, simple though it may be. Louis Pasteur said, "A little science estranges men from God, but much science leads them back to Him." Sir Isaac Newton, perhaps the greatest of scientists, said, "This most beautiful system of the sun, planets, and comets could only proceed from the counsel and dominion of an intelligent and powerful Being."

In a recent article published by American Atheists, Inc., the heart of atheism in America was laid bare, and it was observed to have a terminal disease. This article was written by a particularly zealous (but somewhat discouraged) atheist, who is a graduate of the University of Texas and the president of American Atheists. He related the five basic coronary problems that plague contemporary atheists in the U.S.

The first dilemma he cites within the stricken body of unbelievers is a lack of unity. He begins by noting how unified Christians seem in their stand against abortion, and in the fact that they don't openly criticize one another. Then he says history has shown atheistic attitudes toward each other have consisted of "outright hostility…the Atheists [he uses caps] hate the agnostics, who hate the humanists, who cannot stand the rationalists, who keep their distance from the realists, who will not speak to the Unitarians, and on and on it goes…They cannot even agree on the simple concept that 'there is no god'" (as is the normal practice with professing atheists, he uses lowercase for God).

The second symptom of the diseased heart of atheism in

America, as mentioned in the article, is a lack of zeal. The author says, "Atheists will simply not get involved with the promotion of their chosen lifestyle. I cannot think of a group harder to motivate...Atheists seem to feel that their position with regard to religion is a deeply personal thing that does not need to be shared with others."

How can an atheist share with others something he doesn't have? I suppose it is hard to be an enthusiastic atheist, when the word "enthusiasm" comes from the Greek words *en* and *theos*—meaning "in God."

The third dilemma he mentions is a lack of faith. He admits, "I have met many Atheists who cannot surpass the 'What if I am wrong?' stage." They doubt their doubts.

The fourth ailment of the society of atheists is a lack of boldness. The author remarks about an incident where a newspaper reporter approached him to do an article on the subject of atheistic lifestyles. However, he found nothing but the "fear of man" in those whom he contacted. He said he called "from person to person" and encountered "such deep-seated fear that I could hardly believe my ears...In short, most of the Atheists I contacted were petrified with fear at being found out...It was a climate of total fear."

Finally, he found that the average atheist was bound by a lack of giving. He speaks of generous Christians and then protests, "I know that certainly there are persons of great means who are Atheists, but they simply will not assist in the struggle against religion...And I know you are out there..." He believes that they are out there, somewhere. Theirs is one existence that it is not convenient for him to deny.

It seems that the heart of atheism in the United States has been surviving on a wing and a prayer. Now the beat has stopped. Sadly for their leader, unless some sort of revival takes place, his frantic efforts at CPR will be futile.

Chapter Three

SEEING IS BELIEVING

T HE EXISTENCE OF God is what's known as an "axiom"—
a self-evident truth. The fact that parallel lines never
meet is what's known as an axiom. If I were to devote my life
to trying to either prove or disprove that parallel lines never
meet, I would lack common sense. If the lines meet they are
not parallel, and if they are parallel they will never meet.
This is so obvious that it doesn't need to be proved or disproved. It is self-evident—an axiom.

The existence of God is an axiom. It is obvious that if
there is a creation, there must be a Creator. For things to be
"made," logic, reason, intellect, and rationalism demand that
there is a Maker. This should need to be neither proved nor
disproved.

Let's presume you don't believe because you can't *see*
God. Your philosophy is that "seeing is believing." If that is
so, the next time you see water shimmering on a hot road,
stop for a drink. Or the next time you watch a sunrise and
see the sun move across the sky, remind yourself that your
eyes are lying to you. The sun does not rise, move, or set. It
remains stationary while the earth turns. The next time you
gaze at a blue sky, tell your eyes that they are not seeing correctly. The sky has no color—ask any astronaut. It's an illu-
sion. Sleight-of-hand magicians make their living on the fact
that seeing isn't believing.

We believe in many things we can't see. For example,

right behind you, beside you, and even right in front of you are masses of invisible television signals. Cowboys, Indians, news anchors, soap opera characters, etc., are passing before your eyes. You can't see them; they are totally invisible. If I denied their existence because I couldn't see them, would that alter the reality that they exist? Of course not.

Back to da Vinci

Why do you believe a painting has a painter? Isn't it purely because of the existence of the painting? Do you insist on *seeing* da Vinci before you believe that the Mona Lisa was painted? One could reasonably argue that there may have been another painter, but never that there was *no* painter.

Do you insist on *seeing* the builder before you believe that the house you are in was built? Is that your criteria for belief? I doubt it. Again, the building is ample proof that there was a builder.

Does the jumbo jet have no maker until you lay your eyes on those who assembled the aircraft? Consider for a moment the mechanical intricacies of the plane. Think of the technologically brilliant minds of the people who make them. Yet the human eye leaves man's most complex creations, including the jumbo jet, in the dust of primitive technology. The most brilliant minds on earth cannot begin to recreate an eye. If you lose one, the best modern science can do is give you a glorified marble to slip in the slot. We are still in the dark about its incredible workings. Do you realize that each eye you are currently using has 40 million nerve endings? If you have the brain power to make one nerve ending, tell modern science so that they can begin to see their way to making their first eye.

The fact is, we can't make *anything* from nothing. Find the most brilliant scientist on God's earth, put him in a laboratory, and ask him to make something from nothing. He can't do it. He doesn't know how. We can *re-create*, but we cannot create. We can't even make one grain of sand from nothing. If that is the case, how could we even begin to think for a moment that all of creation—the human body, animals, flowers, birds, trees, fruits, the seasons, the sun, the moon, the stars, etc.—fell together (from nothing) by mere random chance?

Albert Knew

Meditate for a moment on how the seasons of summer, fall, winter, and spring come around each year in the same order. Scientists can predict the sunrise one hundred years from now with incredible accuracy—*to the precise second*. Think of the earth, spinning as it orbits the sun, while our moon orbits the earth. Think of the moon pulling the tides of the sea in and out all over the earth, or the plants taking in carbon dioxide, then giving out oxygen for us to breathe in, and us giving out carbon dioxide for them to take in. Meditate on the sun evaporating seawater, clouds forming, being blown by the invisible wind, rising over the mountains, dropping rain to give life to the earth, and at the same time clearing the air of its impurities. Think of how the mountains hold much of the water in the form of snow, until the heat of summer melts it. Then it feeds the rivers, to water the land and pour into the sea; and so the incredible and predictable cycle of life continues.

I am amazed at the number of people deceived into thinking that because they don't believe in something, it therefore doesn't exist. If a blind man doesn't believe in color, does color not exist? His belief has no bearing whatsoever on its reality. It exists whether he believes in it or not.

If you can't believe in things that you've never seen, how

then do you know you have a brain? You've never seen it. If you can look at this miraculous creation and insist that there's no Creator, then you'd also have to say there's no evidence that your brain exists. Nowhere does the Bible set out to prove that God exists. It just frankly states the obvious: "The fool has said in his heart, 'There is no God'" (Psalm 14:1). That's why we have a bumper sticker, "National Atheist Day—April 1st."

> ATHEISM IS COMPLETELY THE OPPOSITE OF WHAT IT PROFESSES TO BE.

While it is not my purpose to offend you, I want to show you that atheism is completely the opposite of what it professes to be. What is your IQ? Is it 100, or 120? Or do you have an even higher intelligence? Is your IQ around the 140 mark? Do you qualify for work at NASA? Or maybe you approach the intelligence level of Albert Einstein. Listen to Einstein, one of the greatest minds ever made: "Everyone who is seriously interested in the pursuit of science becomes convinced that a spirit is manifest in the laws of the universe—a spirit vastly superior to man, and one in the face of which our modest powers must feel humble."

In *A Brief History of Time*, the highly esteemed evolutionist Stephen Hawking wrote, "It would be very difficult to explain why the universe should have begun in just this way, except as the act of a God who intended to create beings like us." He also said, "Then we shall . . . be able to take part in the discussion of the question of why it is that we and the universe exist. If we find the answer to that, it would be the ultimate triumph of human reason—for then we would know the mind of God."

Perhaps the name "God" offends you. Well, let's put it

aside for a moment and call it a force, a higher power, or like Einstein, "a spirit." Isn't it true that whatever or whoever made this universe must be awesome, to say the least? What sort of supreme creative force could make something as incredible as the sun? The sun's radius is 432,169 miles, 109 times as large as the earth's. If the sun were hollow, a million earths could fit inside it. The temperature of the outer, visible part of the sun is an estimated 9950°F.

Its average distance from earth is 93 million miles, yet light from the sun takes about eight minutes to reach us. Earth would not have any life on it without the sun's energy, which reaches us as heat and light to warm our days and illuminate our world. All plant and animal life relies on the sun's presence. This creative force placed it 93 million miles from us so that it's just warm enough to maintain life. If it were a little closer, we would all die either from its heat or from drowning. In fact, if the polar ice caps were to melt and flood the earth, the sea level would rise high enough to submerge the Empire State Building up to the twentieth floor. If the sun were slightly further away, however, we would all freeze to death. It is said that the energy given off by the sun in one second is approximately 13 million times greater than the average amount of electricity used each year in the entire United States. What sort of creative force could make that sun, then hold it in space and sustain its brilliance? Take a moment to meditate on that thought.

How could this power make the human heart and blood, form the ribs within the body of an unborn baby, make a human eye, or create the flesh that covers our body? How could it create the human mind with its unending, complex corridors, its deepest thoughts and desires? The brain is utterly incredible. It makes you think...doesn't it?

Chapter Four

STRAWBERRIES
AND GARLIC

D O YOU REALIZE that you sneeze at 120 miles per hour? Did you also know that every time you sneeze, you have been programmed to close your eyes? Where does your hair grow from? How can the thin layer of skin on your head send out a special type of hair? It has been instructed by your genes to generate a certain type of hair for the scalp— hair different from that which grows on the arms or legs, or on the eyelids or the eyebrows. Imagine if you had eyebrows or eyelashes that grew to the length of the hair on your head. Think of the fine row of hair that makes up the eyelash or of the way the hairs face the same direction on the eyebrow.

Have you ever studied the ordinary garden snail and wondered how its shell is able to grow in proportion to its body? When it's a baby snail, it has a baby shell. As it doubles in size, it doesn't discard its shell. The hard shell also doubles in size. Do you credit the snail with having a mind brilliant enough to make its own shell? How does a grubby little caterpillar get rid of all its legs while inside a cocoon, grow two fresh ones, then form itself into a butterfly with a slender body and beautiful wings? Perhaps you could mumble "evolution," and believe that it could happen if millions of years were involved. But all this happens in a few weeks.

Do you give an infant credit for having the ability to grow its own teeth? How did you grow both sets of yours? If you ever decide to get false teeth, will you have them made or will you wait for "chance" to make a pair for you? Look at your fingernails. Where did they grow from? What makes up their substance? Look at how your hands are holding this book. Notice how the fingers cradle it, while the thumb holds the pages. One thumb comes from the right side, the other from the left. Both thumbs bend forward. If they bent the other way, you couldn't hold the book. Hands have been designed for the purpose of holding. Sir Isaac Newton said, "In absence of any other proof, the thumb alone would convince me of God's existence."

How is it that your lungs keep breathing irrespective of your will? You have been doing it without a second thought while you have been looking at your thumbs. In fact, becoming conscious of your breathing can hinder the process. Lungs seem to work best without *any* thought from the mind. How does your subconscious mind continually feed you with thoughts, even when you sleep? Listen to it talk to you and keep you company. It never stops. Try to stop it yourself. Put this book down and think of nothing for five minutes. I bet you can't. Your subconscious mind has been set in motion, and it has little to do with your will.

Right at this moment, your liver, kidneys, heart, pancreas, salivary glands, etc., are all working to keep your body alive and functioning. You don't even have the power to switch them off and on. During your sleep tonight, your heart will pump seventy-five gallons of blood through your body each hour.

Contrary to common belief, your lungs are more than just bags to breathe smoke into. They are designed to filter oxygen out of the air you breathe. These organs contain 300 *billion* tiny blood vessels called capillaries. Red blood cells inside the capillary release oxygen, which passes through the capillary wall and into the surrounding tissue. The tissue releases its waste products, like carbon dioxide, which pass through the wall and into the red blood cells. Your entire blood supply washes through your lungs once every minute.

Evolution and Blood

Platelets in your blood play an important role in preventing blood loss by beginning a chain reaction that results in clotting. As blood begins to flow from a cut or scratch, platelets respond to help the blood clot and to stop the bleeding after a short time.

Platelets promote the clotting process by clumping together and forming a plug at the site of a wound and then releasing proteins called "clotting factors." These proteins start a series of chemical reactions that are extremely complicated. Every step of the clotting must go smoothly if a clot is to form. If one of the clotting factors is missing or defective, the clotting process does not work. A serious genetic disorder known as hemophilia results from a defect in one of the clotting factor genes. Because hemophiliacs lack one of the clotting factors, they may bleed uncontrollably from even small cuts or scrapes.

To form a blood clot requires twelve specific individual chemical reactions in the blood. If evolution were true, if this twelve-step process didn't happen in the first generation (i.e., if any one of these specific reactions failed to operate in their exact reaction and order), no creatures would have survived. They all would have bled to death!

In his book *Darwin's Black Box*, biochemistry professor Michael J. Behe, an evolutionist, acknowledges a "powerful challenge to Darwinian evolution"—something he refers to as "irreducible complexity." He gives a simple example: the humble mouse-trap. The mousetrap has five major components that make it functional. If any one of these components is missing, it will not function. It becomes worthless as a mousetrap. Charles Darwin admitted, "If it could be demonstrated that any complex organ existed which could not possibly have been formed by numerous, successive, slight modifications, my theory would absolutely break down" (*The Origin of Species*). If we just take the human eye, one small part of an incredibly complex creation, we will see this same principle of irreducible complexity. The eye cannot be reduced to anything less than what it is. It has thousands of co-equal functions to make it work. If we take away just one of those functions, the rest of the eye is worthless as an eye. How then did the eye evolve when all functions had to be present at once to give it any worth at all?

A Statistical Monstrosity

Perhaps the greatest proof of the Creator's existence is seen when you gaze into the mirror. Your eyes have focusing muscles that move an estimated 100,000 times each day. Each eye has within it a retina that covers less than a square inch and contains 137 million light-sensitive cells. Even a wide-eyed Charles Darwin said, "To suppose that the eye could have been formed by natural selection, seems, I freely confess, absurd in the highest degree."[5]

Your brain contains 10 billion neurons or microscopic nerve cells. Your stomach, which produces four pints of gastric juice each day, has 35 million glands lining it. The next time you eat a delicious meal, be thankful for the 8,000 taste buds that were put into your mouth. Imagine how boring eating would be without them.

The famous statistician George Gallup said, "I could prove God statistically. Take the human body alone: the chance that all the functions of the individual would just happen is a statistical monstrosity." Sir Fred Hoyle, professor of astronomy at Cambridge University, made a similar finding: "The chance that higher life forms might have emerged in this way is comparable to the chance that a tornado sweeping through a junkyard might assemble a Boeing 747 from the materials therein." He concluded, "The likelihood of the formation of life from inanimate matter is one out of $10^{40,000}$...It is big enough to bury Darwin and the whole theory of evolution. There was no primeval soup, neither on this planet nor on any other, and if the beginnings of life were not random, they must therefore have been the product of purposeful intelligence."

Was it an accident that your ears were designed to capture sound? The grooves, bumps, and ridges are made to catch passing sound waves and channel them into the eardrum. Again, your hands were made to grip and feel. The tongue was made to taste food and to shape speech. The nose was made to smell. What if your ears faced backwards, or your nose was upside down (what a nightmare in a rainstorm), or your mouth had two tongues? I am serious. If humanity just happened (with no purposeful design), why don't we see such creatures? In fact, we see the very opposite. From the teeth of a dog to the legs of a grasshopper, one can see practical design in everything that has been made. Despite the evident design around us, those who we assume to be intellectuals show that they are somewhat lacking in common sense: "New scientific revelations about supernovas, black holes, quarks, and the big bang even suggest to some scientists that there is a 'grand design' in the universe" (*U.S. News & World Report*, March 31, 1997). A *child* can see that there is "grand design" in creation.

Now, if an incredibly brilliant creative "force" made all things, then it is not only infinitely more intelligent than man whom it made, but it is surely familiar with what it has made. Not only did it create every one of the 100,000 hairs on the average non-bald human head, but it is also familiar with each individual hair. If the force can make the eye, it is not blind itself.

Creation reflects the genius of the creative Force's hand. Let's look at a common cow. Someone once said, "How is it that a brown cow eats green grass, which turns into white milk, then is made into yellow butter and orange cheese, which are eaten by a person who grows red hair and has blue eyes?" Think of how grass cuttings become milk, cheese, and butter—all from a little stirring and churning. Imagine if you were able to invent a machine that could turn your grass into milk. Yet the cow does just that. Tell me how she does it. If it is so simple, make your millions by inventing a machine that turns grass into milk. Call it a "Lawn Mooer." The cow does it with little effort. Is she wiser than you?

Explain to me how a sparrow knows he is a sparrow and stays with other sparrows, or how a baby knows how to look into the eyes of its mother when no one has taught it to do so. Explain how a tree growing on a steep hillside grows upward and not at right angles to the cliff. Tell me how strawberries can grow next to garlic, and yet both derive their own unique tastes from the same soil and water. How was a wasp made so that its wings beat 100 times every second, or the housefly at 190 times every second, or the mosquito at an amazing 500 beats every second?

The most godless person must be humbled with a sense of awe and wonder when standing beneath the mighty power of Niagara Falls, gazing into the Grand Canyon, or staring into the infinity of space. How much more should we be humbled by the Maker of these things?

Chapter Five

STRONGER THAN THE SEX DRIVE

YEARS AGO, I knew a non-Christian man in his twenties whose doctor told him that he had six months to live. His friends advised him to visit a few prostitutes and enjoy the last six months of his life. He wasn't interested. He found that deep within his heart he had something far stronger than the sex drive. It was his will to live. A cry came from the depths of his being, "Oh, I don't want to die!" I'm sure every one of us can identify with that. No one in his right mind wants to die. That cry is God-given. The Bible tells us that God has put eternity in our hearts.

I once dropped a friend off at the local crematorium (he was alive at the time). As I sat in my car, I couldn't help noticing how pleasantly they had decorated and arranged the area. It was surrounded by a clean block wall, complete with a rose garden in front of the wall. Behind the wall was an inviting pathway leading to open doors. The establishment was no longer called a "mortuary" but was fondly known by most locals as "The Crem." The decor inside was extremely tasteful. The funeral directors (no longer called "undertakers") didn't wear black, but a restrained green. The hearse was called a "coach." Words were carefully chosen so as not to offend anyone. The "graveyard" was referred to as a "cemetery." The person hadn't died; he had deceased. The "coffin," which was called a "casket," was elegantly surrounded by a frill, similar to that on a birthday cake.

When your "death day" comes, you get your own polished casket, your own tidy little plot of ground, with a personal nameplate and your own little rose bush—*kinda makes you look forward to your turn, doesn't it?* No, no! A thousand times, no! It doesn't matter how much death is dressed up, no one in his right mind wants to try it on for size.

Rock Around the Clock

Recently I struck up a conversation with a tall, good-looking surfer from Australia. After getting to know him, I swung the discussion around to Christian things. He was very open. He even shared something with me that he hadn't told another soul. He'd been out on his surfboard when a friend had casually said, "See that big rock over there? That'll be here a thousand years after we're dead and gone." This young man had been so shaken by the gravity of the thought that he paddled in and sat soberly on the beach for twenty minutes. How could a dumb, unthinking, inanimate object such as a rock still be around thousands of years after he died?

Such solemn thoughts are the beginnings of an awakened mind. My first thoughts in that direction came to me when I was about seven years old. My brother took me to see a movie about the French Revolution. Rich people were taken from prison, tied hand and foot by bloodthirsty, murderous peasants, and paraded through the streets of Paris. Then they were cruelly mocked, pushed to the guillotine, and their heads chopped off.

Around the "chopper" sat the ugliest hags I'd ever seen. I watched wide-eyed as each time a head rolled, they would scream with sheer delight, grin a toothless grin, then knit another stitch on their scarves to keep count. The scarves were ten or fifteen feet long.

It made me think how horrible it would be to be waiting

in prison to die. Yet as time progressed, I saw that I too was on death row. With all of humanity, I awaited execution. Our holding cell is rather large, with a blue roof, good ventilation, and bright lighting. We can move around this vast earth and enjoy its pleasures if we wish, but we are all still waiting for the "chopper" to come down. Andy Williams struck a note of truth when he sang, "Ain't it true, no matter what you do, they're gonna bury you, beneath the cold, cold ground. Big or tall, or long or short, or fat or small—it's gonna get you all." The Bible gives the reason for this. God, the Judge of the universe, has proclaimed the death sentence upon all humanity: "The soul who sins shall die" (Ezekiel 18:20). Proof of our sin will be our death.

Playing Chicken

My associate, Mark Spence, and I were once driving to an airport on a country road, just south of Grand Rapids, Michigan. As we rounded a curve at 60 mph, a woman suddenly drove her car from a busy side street directly in front of our vehicle. We were so close to her that I could see the look of terror in her eyes. Mark had no time to think. He instinctively swerved to the left to miss the woman's car. Our tires screeched as we crossed the yellow line into oncoming traffic. He had a split second to make a decision to drive into her car (and no doubt kill the woman) or swing into oncoming traffic. He did the latter, found a gap, and back we swerved half a second later onto the right side of the road.

If the incident had happened an instant later, we would surely have been killed and missed our flight (I hate missing flights). Both of us realized how close we had brushed with death, and duly thanked God that we had averted a horrible accident.

While I often tell crowds that it is a fact of life that tomorrow any one of us could be dead, we don't really believe that. Death is something that happens to *other* people. In 1971, health author Jerome Rodale said, "I'm going to live to be one hundred." He died the next day at the age of fifty-one. I'm sure he was surprised that he died. If each of us could truly comprehend that tomorrow we could be in eternity, we would take more seriously the claims of the Bible.

A town once had a portion of road on which there were continual fatalities. Drivers, despite warning signs, would speed around a corner and be killed. Finally, one of the local councilmen had a bright idea. He suggested putting a flock of chickens on the side of the road. They did, and fatalities dramatically dropped. The drivers slowed down for the sake of the chickens.

PLENTY OF PEOPLE AVOID TAXES; NOBODY AVOIDS DEATH.

It would seem that the speeders saw the danger of speed for chickens, but not for themselves. Why? Because inherent within each of us is this senseless idea that "it will never happen to me." It's always the other guy who gets killed; it's always the other guy who gets cancer. But I am sure that every person who died before us had the "I never thought it would happen to me" attitude.

A friend once refused to put on a car seat belt, saying, "I'm not planning to have an accident." I told him that was one of the world's dumbest statements. There has never been a "planned" accident. If it is an accident, it is not planned. If it's planned, it's not an accident. The dictionary says an accident is "anything occurring unexpectedly." Sadly, that's the way death comes to most.

While I was open-air preaching, I was heckled for many years by a man named Willie. Almost daily, he would say,

"When I see God, I'm going to spit in His face! Then I'm going to say, 'What about this !@%!* Ray Comfort!'" One day Willie dropped dead. At a young age, he had a heart attack and died. I know that he also had the attitude that it would never happen to him. Much to his shock (and mine), Willie is now in eternity.

Someone once said, "There are only two things in life that are sure—death and taxes." That's not true. Plenty of people avoid taxes; nobody avoids death. We are all part of the ultimate statistic: ten out of ten die. The leading actor of a popular TV series put it this way: "Death is a guarantee from the day we are born. But I guess we don't think about it because we think it will never happen." How right he is.

A Pulled Plug

The incredible thing about God's promise of eternal life is that He backs it up with His Holy Spirit to show us that He means what He says. Just as you could prove the reality of electricity by experiencing an electric shock, so God's promises carry a punch with them. If you refuse to believe in electricity, put a fork in an electrical outlet. Suddenly you will become a believer, because you have experienced the power.

The Bible tells us that when the gospel is preached, it comes "in power, and in the Holy Spirit and in much assurance" (1 Thessalonians 1:5). The reason you can walk around on God's earth, breathing God's air, seeing God's flowers, His birds, His trees, His sun—and yet not be aware of Him —is that you are spiritually dead. You are like an appliance with the plug pulled out.

We are made up of three main parts: body, soul, and spirit. The body is the machine we walk around in. It is fearfully and wonderfully made. Our soul is our self-conscious part—the area of the emotions, the will, and the conscience.

But our spirit is our God-conscious part. If you are not aware of God, it is because your receiver is dead. That's why I went for twenty-two years without giving God two seconds of serious thought. My reasoning about eternity was merely in the natural realm. I was completely "without understanding." Yet from the moment I was plugged in, on April 25, 1972, I have been aware that "in Him we live and move and have our being" (Acts 17:28).

No Greater Insult

The key that unlocks the door of salvation is faith. The Bible tells us that without faith it is impossible to please God (see Hebrews 11:6). Try having a relationship with someone and see if you can establish any sort of friendship without faith. Walk up to a woman and introduce yourself. When she tells you her name, say, "I don't believe you." Watch her reaction. When she tells you where she lives, say you don't believe that either. Carry on like that for a while, and before long you may be nursing a black eye. Your lack of faith in her is a strong insinuation that she is a liar. The command of the Scriptures is, "Have faith in God" (Mark 11:22). If a meaningful human relationship can't be established without faith, what sort of relationship could you expect to have with God, if by your unbelief you continue to call Him a liar? Martin Luther stated, "What greater insult can there be to God...than not to believe His promises?"

How Does He Get In?

Imagine you had never seen a television set. As you take your first look at one, your hand runs across the smooth glass screen. "Push the button and you will see a person reading the news," I say with an air of pride at the miracle of modern technology. You smile and ask, "How does he get in there?"

"Well, he's not actually in the box." Your smile broadens as you ask, "Is he in there or isn't he?" "You don't understand. What happens is that unseen television signals are transmitted through the air. They are then picked up by what is called an antenna or receiver and sent down wires through electrical impulses into this plug, along this cord, and into the set."

The tone of your voice changes. "Do you expect me, a rational, logical human being, to believe that this newsreader of yours floats invisibly through the air until he comes to your antenna, slides down it, through those wires, up the cord and into this box to read the news? Come on, what do you take me for—a fool?"

I smile and say, "I know it sounds preposterous, but all you have to do to prove what I say is to push the button. The set will automatically come on." Despite the fact that your logic makes me seem like a fool, there is an air of confidence in my voice because what I have said is provable.

> THERE IS NO DENIAL—THE CLAIM OF CHRISTIANITY IS TRULY FANTASTIC.

There is no denial—the claim of Christianity is truly fantastic. It maintains that the invisible God of creation can supernaturally reveal Himself to you. Despite the fact that it is illogical, I have more than an air of confidence because what I am saying *is* provable. May I say, with all due respect, stop tapping the screen in skepticism. Push the button...if you dare. I know you can offer a hundred reasons why it shouldn't work, but push the button. Or do you have an ulterior motive? Perhaps it's not that you *can't* find God, but that you *won't*. If you refuse to reach out and press the button of "repentance toward God and faith toward our Lord Jesus Christ," then you are choosing to remain in willful ignorance of the truth.

Chapter Six

ATHEIST OBSTACLES

A FAVORITE ARGUMENT of the atheist is that God's existence cannot be *disproved*. This is true. As mentioned earlier, one needs to be omniscient to disprove God's existence. However, one should also be *omnipresent* (dwelling everywhere at once) to be absolutely sure that God doesn't exist (although it could argued that one who is totally omniscient wouldn't have to be omnipresent).

It is because the atheist is neither omniscient nor omnipresent that he then takes an illogical leap by concluding that there is no God, *because it cannot be proven that He doesn't exist*. Such reasoning is absurd. Why would anyone try to prove that God *doesn't* exist when it can be proven that He *does*? Creation proves scientifically and absolutely to any sane mind that there is a Creator. His existence is axiomatic.

The atheist also has a problem with both answered and unanswered prayer. Here's a scenario that no doubt happens daily somewhere in the world. A young boy becomes deathly ill. The entire family gathers for prayer. However, despite earnest and sincere prayer, the child tragically dies. Their explanation for the death is that God took him to heaven because He wanted the child there. That's seen by the atheist as "unanswered prayer." Or the child miraculously makes a recovery, which the family hails as an evident miracle. God obviously answered the family's prayers by saving the child from death. The atheist maintains that it wasn't answered prayer but that the child recovered because his body healed itself.

Was the recovery a miracle? Perhaps. Then again, perhaps it wasn't. Only God knows. The fact is that we have no idea what happened. However, one thing we do know is that answered or unanswered prayer has nothing to do with God's existence. Let me explain. I have a Dodge Caravan. Let's say it has a problem. What would be my intellectual capacity if I concluded that it had no manufacturer simply because I couldn't contact them about the dilemma? The fact of their existence has nothing to do with whether or not they return my calls.

Neither does God's existence have anything to do with the fact that there are those who have experienced miracles, seen visions, or supposedly heard His voice. The sun doesn't exist because we see its light, or because we feel its warmth. Its existence has nothing to do with any human testimony. Nor does it cease to exist because a blind man is not aware of its reality, or because it becomes cloudy, or the night falls. The sun exists, period.

God's existence isn't dependent on the Bible or its authenticity, the existence of the Church, the prophets, or even creation. God existed before the Scriptures were penned, before creation came into existence. Even if the Bible was proved to be fraudulent, God would still exist.

Adamant atheist April Pedersen writes, "The human trait of seeking comfort through prayer is a strong one."[6] This is true. However, April fails to see that human nature itself is very predictable. If men will not embrace the biblical revelation of God, their nature is to go into idolatry. "Idolatry" is the act of creating a god in our image, whether it is shaped with the human hands (a physical "idol"), or shaped in the human mind through the imagination. Those who create their own god then use it as a "good-luck charm" to do their bidding. The idolater uses his god for his own ends. He calls on his god to win a football game, a boxing match, the lottery, and, of course, to win a war. Idolatry is as predictable as it is illogical.

Idolaters, of which there are billions throughout the world, are deceived into thinking that their imaginary god really does exist. They assume that Almighty God changes like pliable putty to whatever they visualize Him to be. Such a thought is ludicrous. It is like standing before an oncoming steam roller and imagining it to be cotton candy. Our imaginings don't change reality. God doesn't change just because we change our perception of Him. The Bible says, "I am the LORD, I do not change" (Malachi 3:6). However, there is something that is even more ludicrous than the imaginings of idolaters. It is that trait of human nature that is just as predictable—the intellectual suicide of the atheist.

> EVEN IF THE BIBLE WAS PROVED TO BE FRAUDULENT, GOD WOULD STILL EXIST.

The question arises as to the legitimacy of the atheist's obstacles. Let me share an analogy to clarify this. One moonless night, unbeknown to the passengers of a plane, hijackers broke into the cockpit. They violently took over the controls, contacted the control tower, and demanded that the White House release a large number of political prisoners. When authorities refused to comply with the demands, the terrorists threatened to fire on the passengers and force them out of an open door at 20,000 feet.

During negotiations, the captain was able to scribble a note on official paper warning of the hijackers' threat and telling each passenger to reach under his seat. There they would find a parachute which they were instructed to put on immediately.

As the note was passed from passenger to passenger, there were different reactions. Some saw the note was obviously authentic as it was written on official paper. Besides, they remembered the strange jolt when the hijackers violently took control of the plane. They immediately put the parachute on realizing that they had nothing to lose but their pride if the note was fraudulent, and everything to gain if it was true.

Some passengers refused to believe the note because they thought there was no way that there could be a parachute beneath the seat. They were so sure of this fact that they didn't even check.

A couple rejected the note because they noticed a passenger who had only pretended to put the parachute on. They could see that he hadn't bothered to tighten the straps.

Others laughed at the note as though it were some joke, while others didn't bother reading it because they were watching an onboard movie.

Some passengers even ignored the evidence of the official paper and the jolt of the plane, and instead maintained that they believed that the plane didn't have a pilot and that there was no aircraft maker. As far as they were concerned it came together by accident, taking millions of years.

Suddenly, the hijackers burst into the darkened cabin, thrust open the exit doors, and began firing automatic weapons over the terrified passengers' heads, forcing them to jump 20,000 feet into the blackness. Most fell to their deaths. However, those who had had the good sense to believe and obey the captain were saved from such a horrible demise.

Here's the analogy: There is nothing wrong with questioning the mystery of prayer, the authenticity of the Bible, the existence of God, and the fact of hypocrisy. However, it is wise to put on the "parachute" first. Reach under your seat and put it on. Do what the "Note" says—"Put on the Lord Jesus Christ" (Romans 13:14). The parachute is either there or it isn't. After you have secured your own eternal salvation, then you can worry about the fate of the pretender. If you think it's important, you can then try to figure out the age of the earth, etc.

This is the teaching of the Bible: "Seek first the kingdom of God and His righteousness, and all these things shall be added to you" (Matthew 6:33). Once you have done that, my hope is that you will spend your time making sure that those around you have seen that Note and obeyed its sobering instruction. Have you put on the Lord Jesus Christ? You could be made to jump through the door of death into a black and horrifying eternity at any moment. There is a merciless Law waiting for you—a Law far harsher than the law of gravity. You desperately need the Savior. Please, don't put off your eternal salvation for another moment.

Chapter Seven

WORMS
TRANSFORMED

I MAGINE YOUR reaction if you turned on the television to hear the following news item:

Scientists have just invented a machine that is able to turn your kitchen waste into a small, edible packet of food. It is surrounded by a white, hygienically sealed protective casing. When this packet is opened, the contents may be eaten in a variety of delicious ways. It doesn't matter what type of food waste is put into the machine at night, it always comes out the same consistent yellow and white color the next morning. If fat, spinach, bread crusts, apple cores, wheat, and even live grubs and worms are put into it, all are miraculously transformed overnight into a delicious-tasting food by the next morning.

Excited scientists report that this incredible machine will have the ability to reproduce itself. Believe it or not, it can make a special hygienically sealed packet, which produces (you guessed it) another food-making machine. At any time, any of these machines themselves can be easily dismantled, cooked, and eaten. They are said to taste "finger-lickin' good."

I'm sure that most of us would view such a news item with great skepticism, yet that is what we have with the ordinary, common, everyday chicken. Each day, most of the 4 billion chicken brains do what modern man's brain can't. They make eggs and chickens. Is the chicken more intelligent than man? Probably not. Therefore, something far superior to man must have made the chicken. "Accident" is the alternative.

Aristotle said, "God, having become unseen to every nature, through His works is seen." Plato said, "The world must have a cause, and that cause is the Eternal Maker." Cicero echoed, "What can be so clear when we look at the sky and the heavenly bodies is that there is some deity of surpassing mind by whom these are governed."

Made for Each Other

Without getting into blushing territory, think how in almost all of creation the male and the female are made for each other. From dogs and elephants, to birds and bees, to man, each is designed for reproduction. Like a nut and a bolt, they are made to fit together perfectly. For the male dog to have been made without a maker—that is, to believe that "chance" threw together its legs, brain, muscles, heart, liver, lungs, skin, eyes, and ears, not to mention its reproductive organs—is unthinkable. But to add to this thought that it just so happened that a causeless accident also threw together the female dog, with its legs, brain, muscles, heart, etc.—and just happened to throw in the necessary complementary reproductive parts—is nothing short of insane. It is intellectual suicide. It is to have brain liposuction. Yet the professing atheist holds to this belief.

THE MALE AND FEMALE HAVE BEEN MADE WITH PURPOSE IN MIND.

Add to these thoughts the fact that there are hundreds of different species of dogs, all with both male and female organs. If they didn't have both sexes, dogs wouldn't be with us today. The first male would have been the last male. Think of all the different types of animals: lion, tiger, elephant, bear, horse, cow, cat, camel, giraffe, zebra, etc. Notice how each of them has two eyes, two specially designed ears, a brain, one mouth, one tongue, specially designed teeth, taste buds, one heart, kidneys, a pancreas, a liver, etc., as well as male and female, each having appropriate reproductive parts. Think of all the different birds: sparrow, dove, chicken, canary, kiwi, eagle, hawk, peacock, etc. Notice how they too have been given two eyes, two ears, one brain, a heart, etc., and each has male and female. Fish follow the same pattern. The male and female have been made with purpose in mind. This incredibly consistent order in created life shows a supremely intelligent and ordered mind in the Maker. If you deny that fact, go make a bird. I don't mean a wooden one. I mean a living, breathing, eating, seeing, hearing, reproducing, thinking, whistling, and flying one. And by the way, make it from nothing.

A Coincidence

Imagine that you see me carrying a large bag of oranges to my car. You walk away for a few minutes, then return to hear me say, "Hey, look on the ground. The bag split and all the oranges fell out!" You look on the ground and see forty-five oranges in nine perfect rows of five oranges each. What would be the chance of those oranges (all forty-five of them) "falling" into nine perfectly straight rows of five? For five oranges to fall out of a bag and land in a line would be amazing. But for forty-five to do that is too much for an intelligent mind to believe. Someone with an ordered mind placed them there. Their order tells you that.

I once experimented to see how a human brain would react to ordered coincidence. A huge avocado tree was in the habit of dropping leaves between our back door and my office. One day I noticed seven leaves on the ground, so I bent down and placed them in a perfectly straight line. Then I walked into my office, sat down, and waited for my wife to come in and say what I thought she would say. It was very predictable. She walked in and asked, "Why did you put those leaves like that?" There was no way that her reasoning mind could believe that seven leaves fell off the avocado tree into a straight line. She knew that an intelligent mind (mine) had put them there.

It would be far more logical to say that the epic movie *Ben Hur* happened by accident than to say that there is no God. There was no director, no producer, no sponsors, no film, no cameras, no actors, no makeup artists, no writers ... no chariot race. There was nothing. Zip. Zilch. Then there was a really big bang, and over millions of years the movie came into being.

Imagine that I had a new car, but I had peeled off the maker's nameplate. Would you then think that the car had no maker because you could see neither the maker nor the maker's identity? No, you would know that an intelligent brain designed the vehicle, because it had been made with purpose in mind. Take for instance the windshield. It is clearly more than ornamental. It is a functional part of the car, made to protect the occupants while allowing them to see where they are going. It has been specially fitted with windshield wipers to keep the windshield clear. The manufacturer has even fitted the car with little squirters, so that the windshield may be moistened for easy cleaning. The car has been made with purpose in mind.

Your Maker has given you two "windshields" to see out of. The "wipers" He has fitted are infinitely more sophisticated than any made by a modern car manufacturer. They clean your windshields simultaneously at the incredible speed of 1/500th of a second. The process, which takes place irrespective of your will, happens so quickly that you don't even see it happen. If you are an average person, you have cleaned your windshield approximately sixty times since beginning this chapter. You've even been given little squirters called tear ducts, which squirt clear liquid onto your windshields from the corners of both your eyes, keeping them lubricated so that the wipers can be more effective. Without the tear ducts, the eyes would become dry and affect your vision. Try drinking milk each day and see if the eye lubricant comes out white. Somehow your body filters out the coloring of the liquids you drink, so that the cleaning liquid is clear and doesn't cloud your vision.

Heavy Thoughts

Speaking of clouded vision, I was once looking at clouds from the underside and had a strange thought. I began meditating on the fact that when I clean my car, I often carry a bucket of water to it. The bucket, when filled with water, is very heavy. If water is heavy and clouds are full of water, then clouds *must* be heavy.

The next step was to call weather experts and see if I was correct in my assumption. I explained my thoughts, then asked, "Are clouds heavy?" "Yes, sir," came the firm reply. In fact (at the risk of making you fearful to step outside), the average summer rain cloud weighs hundreds of thousands of tons. When I asked what holds the clouds in the sky, the expert explained that clouds are made of water vapor, which condenses around tiny dust particles. When the water becomes drops, the drops drip. Or to put it more clearly, when the drips form into drops, the drips drop.

The weather expert was full of enthusiasm as he answered my questions. At last, someone was drawing on his expertise. But the moment I mentioned any thought of the cloud Maker, he didn't want to talk any longer. Strange.

Chapter Eight

TOMBSTONE FACE

I DON'T KNOW IF you have noticed, but almost every time there is a massive disaster—a ship sinks or an earthquake kills multitudes, the traditional church (as opposed to the biblical Church) is called upon to bury the dead. I feel saddened that so much of the world equates what the traditional church stands for with biblical Christianity.

A few moments studying the Scriptures should show that there is a vast difference between what "religion" says and what the Bible teaches. Yet hundreds of millions are deceived into thinking that they are one and the same.

Religion is man's self-righteous efforts to reach God. In Jesus Christ, God reached down to man. History has shown that the greatest enemy of Christianity is what is commonly called "organized religion." Jesus was murdered by men who professed to love God but who did not follow His teachings. Throughout the Book of Acts, the established religious leaders opposed the early Christians. No doubt such will be the case at the end of this age. The apostle Paul proclaimed damnation on those who profess to be godly, and yet preach "another gospel" (Galatians 1:6–9).

When the established church is called upon in a disaster, they open the Bible with nauseating predictability to Psalm 23. The page is then dusted, and read in a monotone voice emanating from a tombstone face:

"Yea, though I walk through the valley of the shadow of

death, I will fear no evil…"

It seems that they think that psalm deals with death. In fact, it is the very opposite.

If I stand in the shadow of a wall, I'm not *in* the wall, I'm merely in close proximity to it. If I'm in the shadow of death, I'm not *in* death, I'm merely in close proximity to it.

This life is the shadow of death. Death casts its cold, dark shadow over us every minute of our breathing lives. The Scriptures, speaking of the coming of the Messiah, said, "Those who dwelt in the land of the shadow of death, upon them a light has shined" (Isaiah 9:2). When you come to Jesus Christ, the Light of the World, you no longer "walk in darkness" but have the "Light of life." When someone receives Him who is "the way, the truth, and the life," they don't receive a religion. They receive the very source of life itself. Just as light banishes darkness, so the life we receive banishes death.

A Penny to the Eye

What is at the root of your convictions? For your own sake, ask yourself what *hinders* you from coming to the Savior? Is it your pride? Do you prefer the praises of men to the praise of God? Do you fear man more than you fear God? Perhaps you are afraid your friends will laugh at you. Your acquaintances will; but your friends won't. They will respect you despite your beliefs.

Perhaps it's your love of money. Will you, like the rich man fleeing from a sinking ship, put your gold into your pockets and drown because of its weight? Will you perish because of your riches? Remember when Jim Henson died unexpectedly? He had just sold his Muppet empire to the Disney Corporation for an estimated $100 million. How much did he take with him? There are no pockets in a shroud. A penny held to the eye can blot out the whole of creation.

Years ago, Southern California police carried out an interesting sting operation. They had a list of thousands of wanted criminals who had somehow evaded jail. Instead of risking their lives by attempting to arrest each one, they sent all the criminals a letter telling them they had won a large amount of money in a drawing.

The police put signs and banners on a building, and placed balloons and even a clown on the outside to create a festive atmosphere in order to welcome the "winners." As each criminal entered the building, he heard music and other sounds of celebration. He was then ushered into a room where he smiled as his hand was shaken. The facial expression changed from joy to unbelief as each was told, "Congratulations, you have just won time in prison!" Dozens of criminals made their way through the main doors, were arrested and ushered out the back door.

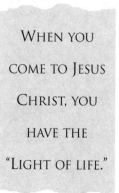

WHEN YOU COME TO JESUS CHRIST, YOU HAVE THE "LIGHT OF LIFE."

It was interesting to note that many of the lawbreakers admitted as they were apprehended, "I *thought* it was a sting operation!" but they couldn't stay away because of their greed. Their love of money blinded them to reason. Don't be like them. Think deeply about the issue of eternity.

Wanted: Eyes

A long time ago, I purchased two Java sparrows for my bird aviary. They were attractive little birds, with smooth gray feathers and brightly colored beaks. As usual, the bird store had placed them in a brown paper bag and stapled the top. It was a workday and some time before I went home, so I cut a small hole in the side of the bag as an air hole and placed it on my office desk.

As the day passed, I was amazed at the pattern of human reaction. Most who stepped into my office wondered why on earth I had a moving paper bag on my desk. When I told them it was a bag of birds, they would pick it up, put their eye to the hole and say, "Wow! What sort of birds are they?" It was at that moment that I would mumble, "Mexican eye-peckers." It was amazing to see how quickly a bag-hole could be pulled away from the eye.

GOD'S DEFINITION OF GOOD IS PERFECTION—IN THOUGHT, WORD, AND DEED.

If we are so quick to care for the eye, how much more should we care for the soul, the very life that looks through the eye?

Imagine if you picked up a newspaper and saw the following advertisement: "Wanted: eyes—must be fresh. Transplant doctor offering $50,000 for one eye, $1,000,000 for a matching pair." All you have to do is go in and let them painlessly remove both of the eyes, and a million dollars is yours! Now you can see the world! No, you can't. If you sell your eyes, you will sit in darkness until the day of your death. Think about it. How much would you sell your eyes for? I am sure that you wouldn't think of it. They are priceless. Yet they are just the windows of your soul. If the eyes are priceless, how much must your soul be worth? The Bible says it is without price. Of all the things that should be supremely important to you, it's not your eyes (or your health) that you should be most concerned about—it is the eternal salvation of your soul.

Good People

When I became a Christian, I found myself in a dilemma. The Bible told me, "There is none who does good, no, not one" (Romans 3:12). Yet I knew many good people. The problem was that God's definition of good and mine were different. We may say a man is "good" because he's stopped stealing and has reformed his ways. We think that good is merely "not bad." God's definition of good is perfection—in thought, word, and deed.

Millions of religious people are striving to be good, believing that will *merit* entrance into heaven. In essence, they are attempting to purchase everlasting life by offering their good deeds to God as an exchange. On Judgment Day, it will not be seen as a mere offer for purchase, but a detestable attempt to bribe the Judge to forget our crimes against His Law.

Do you know of anyone who is "good"? Was Mother Teresa good? No, she said that she needed Jesus Christ as her Savior. Like the rest of us, she had to admit her sins and turn from them (repent). How about Mahatma Ghandi? Was he good? No, he said, "It is a constant torture to me that I am still so far from Him whom I know to be my very life and being. I know it is my own wretchedness and wickedness that keeps me from Him." He acknowledged *his* sins. Perhaps the only good person you can find is yourself. In truth, what we are really doing when we say that there are plenty of good people is attempting to justify our own sins. Let me speak to the wife of any man who says he's perfect. I'm sure that she will tell me the truth.

Chapter Nine

I'LL RESURRECT
HER FOR YOU

D URING THE twelve years I spoke in "Speaker's Corner" in my home city, it became a popular area for public speaking. On a bad day, I would always have at least twenty to thirty listeners. On a good day, it was normal to have 150 listeners, ninety percent of whom were non-Christians. In 1986, however, I found myself on a soapbox on a sidewalk in Hawaii, speaking to a moving congregation—no one would stop. My wife, Sue, and I had flown thousands of miles to speak to about ninety young people from around the world. All week I had spoken on evangelism, and now we were putting it into practice. I had taught on the principles of fishing. Now we were out to sea, but there wasn't a bite in sight.

It was then that I remembered a funeral drama I had written. When I had conducted a number of genuine funerals, I noticed that eyes and ears are wide open when people are listening over the top of a dead loved one. So after a little organizing, I dressed as a priest (people tend to give credibility to someone wearing a uniform). Then I led six black-clad pallbearers, carrying a sheet-covered corpse, down a main street of Honolulu.

As we marched, we were overtaken by a fire engine towing a lifeboat. Suddenly, one member of our group approached me and with wide eyes said, "Someone has drowned at Waikiki—right where we are going to do the drama!" To do it there would have been in bad taste, so I went ahead to tell our "mourners" of the need for relocation. Unbeknown to me, an ex-serviceman was standing on a street corner praying, "God, where are you?" when a "priest" walked by. He rushed after me, grabbed me by the arm and began confessing his heart to me. He was genuinely repentant, so I led him in a prayer of commitment to Christ.

I couldn't find the mourners. They had gone to look for us, so the new convert and I made our way back to where I had left the corpse and the pallbearers. When we arrived, I could hardly get to them because of the crowd. Hundreds of people, *who thought we had the corpse of the person who had drowned at Waikiki*, packed tightly around us. It turned out that no one had drowned; it had been a false alarm, and I preached myself hoarse to a massive crowd for about an hour.

> "MAN WILL BELIEVE ANY-THING, AS LONG AS IT'S NOT IN THE BIBLE."

When we did the same drama in Reno, Nevada, two police cars suddenly pulled up and two policemen came rushing up to me. One of them pointed at the sheet-covered corpse and demanded, "What've you got under there?" I said, "A corpse. I'll resurrect her for you. Little maid, I say to you, 'Arise.'" The teen-age corpse sat up on cue and smiled. The officer burst into laughter and walked off mumbling, "You guys can carry on..."

When we did the same drama in Salt Lake City, I found myself preaching outside a punk-rock joint. We had just gathered a good crowd when an ambulance pulled up, followed by a fire engine and police cars. I wasn't at all alarmed when a policeman pulled me to one side, because it was the ninth time the police had joined in the drama. In a rather firm voice, he too asked what was going on. When I explained what we were doing, he said, "Well, your little drama has just cost Salt Lake City a thousand bucks." Someone had seen us carrying the corpse, thought we had the real thing, and called the emergency department.

Why is it that humanity has to lose a loved one before people stop for a moment and ask what life is about? I have spoken in numbers of universities to so-called radicals, and these pseudo intellectuals know the answer to everything except the issues that really matter. They can tell you what the moon is made of, but they haven't the faintest idea what they are doing here on earth. To them, our origin is a mystery. They know what they are made of, but they don't know what they were made for, or what death holds in store for them. Dimwitted questions such as, "Which came first, the chicken or the egg?" wouldn't even need to be asked if willfully blind humanity opened the Bible at Genesis chapter one. The Bible tells us that the chicken beat the egg.[7] Napoleon was right when he said, "Man will believe anything, as long as it's not in the Bible."

The Assumption

We embrace without question absurd speculations such as Darwin's theory of evolution. Humbling though it is, I must confess that I was once a Darwinist. I too sat in front of a television set and nodded my unthinking head at evolution. I too listened as messy-haired, long-worded scientists told me "fact" after "fact," without an ounce of substantiation. In truth, these imaginative dreamers merely got together with clever creative cartoonists to give us their dreams in drawing form. Face it; there are no facts to back up the tale. Listen to their special language: "We believe, surmise, suspect, think, assume, perhaps, maybe, possibly..." Darwin himself, whose theory has evolved into something he never said, could hardly believe how the world latched on to his speculation. He wrote, "I was a young man with unformed ideas. I threw out queries, suggestions, wondering all the time over everything; and to my astonishment the ideas took like wildfire. People made a religion out of them!" Good choice of words. All you need to be a believer in the religion of evolution is blind faith. Just take everything you are taught about the theory to be gospel truth. H. S. Lipson (Professor of Physics, University of Manchester, UK) said, "In fact, evolution became in a sense a scientific religion; almost all scientists have accepted it and many are prepared to 'bend' their observations to fit in with it."

Look at this newspaper report:

> The study of man's origins have been thrown into turmoil by the discovery that human beings are almost genetically identical to chimpanzees and gorillas. The finding made by biologists overturns the accepted idea that mankind developed separately from apes in the distant past more than twenty million years ago, and have thus developed into very different creatures. The biologists say that the separation took place far more recently—about 5,000,000 years ago. Our ancestry is dramatically shorter than we once supposed, they believe. "We used to think we were cousins of the apes," says Professor David Pilbeam, a Harvard University anthropologist. "Now it is becoming more clear that we are more like brothers and sisters."

We are more like brothers and sisters to apes? That's an insult to apes. Experts say that violence is unknown among the creatures. They are generally gentle. They don't need to be continually policed so that they don't rape and murder, like progressive man.

Maybe your faith rests on "scientific proof" such as carbon dating. *Science* magazine reported, "Shells from living snails were carbon dated as being 27,000 years old" (vol. 224, 1984). A science article in *Time* (June 11, 1990) subtitled "Geologists show that carbon dating can be way off" should show you that scientific proof isn't worthy of your trust.

If you are a believer in evolution, answer this. Did the first fish that crawled out of the ocean to become an animal have lungs or gills? If he had lungs (which were needed to breathe while on land), why did they evolve while he was underwater? If he had only gills (which were needed to survive while underwater), he wouldn't survive on land for more than two minutes. He also has another little problem. He needs to find a "she" who likewise decided to crawl up onto the land at the same time. She too needs to have lungs or she won't survive for two minutes. If he is the only one to make it to shore and to develop lungs, the new species of lungfish will die out when he does.

> ALL YOU NEED TO BE A BELIEVER IN THE RELIGION OF EVOLUTION IS BLIND FAITH.

The Giraffe's Neck

The theory of evolution would have us believe that God didn't make the giraffe with a long neck. Instead, it evolved from a short-necked animal to become a giraffe with an extended neck to reach the leaves on tall trees. As the animal stretched to reach leaves, this stretching effort was somehow imprinted in his genes. When he and his mate had offspring, his stretch genes were passed on to the next generation, and they were therefore born with longer necks. Thus was born the giraffe species. This is supposedly the case with all of creation.

Over millions of years we adapted to our surroundings.[8]

Let me then project where evolution should take the still-evolving species of modern man. Since the advent of modern man, he has used a spoon to eat certain food. If he continues to do so, evolution will do its marvelous work. Mankind, in a few million years, will have a "spoon" evolve (grow) from his right hand (if he is right-handed). This will happen because the spoon usage will be imprinted in his genes, and the spoon genes will be passed down from generation to generation. The spoon-hand extension will make it difficult for him to brush his teeth, but evolution will no doubt solve that problem. If he can train himself to use his left hand to brush his teeth, he will brush an average of around 60,000 times over his lifespan. This will be passed through the genes to the following generations, and his left hand will (over millions of years) grow a flesh-and-blood toothbrush extension. This is no stretch of the imagination. If fish can evolve lungs and legs, and dinosaurs evolve wings, anything is possible... to those who believe.

If I can't convince you of how brainless the theory of evolution is, perhaps the following people can.

Sir Arthur Keith (who wrote the foreword to Darwin's *Origin of the Species*, 100th edition) said, "Evolution is unproved and unprovable. We believe it only because the only alternative is special creation, and that is unthinkable."

Malcolm Muggeridge, the famous British journalist and philosopher, said, "I myself am convinced that the theory of evolution, especially the extent to which it's been applied, will be one of the great jokes in history books of the future."

Dr. T. N. Tahmisian of the U. S. Atomic Energy Commission said, "Scientists who go about teaching that evolution is a fact of life are great con-men, and the story they are telling may be the greatest hoax ever. In explaining evolution, we do not have one iota of fact."

Even *Time* magazine admits, "Scientists concede that their most cherished theories are based on embarrassingly few fossil fragments and that huge gaps exist in the fossil record" (November 7, 1977).

Pigs Have Pigs

Not too many believers in Darwin have looked closely at the theory of evolution. If they did, they would find that the structural pillars are nonexistent: Nebraska Man was "scientifically" built up from one tooth, which was later found to be from a pig. Java Man (found early in the last century) was nothing more than a piece of skull, a fragment of thigh bone, and three molar teeth. The rest was the work of the imagination and plaster of Paris.

Heidelberg Man was built up from a jawbone, a large chin section, and some teeth. Most scientists of the day have rejected it because it's similar to the jawbone found in modern man. Still, many evolutionists believe he's 250,000 years old. And don't look to Neanderthal Man for any evidence of evolution. He died of exposure. His skull was exposed as being fully human, not ape. Not only was his stooped posture found to be caused by disease, but he spoke and was artistic and religious. After Piltdown Man celebrated his 500,000th birthday, his skull turned out to belong to a 600-year-old woman and his jaw to a modern ape. All evidence of Peking Man, who was said to have been around at the time of his friend and neighbor, Piltdown, has completely disappeared. He's been reclassified as human. New Guinea Man dates way back to 1970, while Cro-Magnon Man is described as being "one of the earliest and best established fossils... at least equal in physique and brain capacity to that of modern man" (a small brain). In other words, there's no difference.

Listen to this quote from a television program on the subject of evolution:

> To make any kind of judgment, one has to appreciate how little evidence there is of all our ideas of human evolution...If we were to gather all the material on early human remains, from everywhere on earth, and bring it together in one place, it would scarcely fill a single coffin. There would be room to spare...The gaps are still huge. The missing "link" is more like a missing chain, stretching back longer than the period for which we had human fossils.

Read the quote again. Look at what they are saying: "little evidence," "ideas," "scarcely fill a coffin." Again, well-chosen words. Put the idea in a coffin where it belongs and bury it forever. G. K. Chesterton was so right when he said, "The evolutionists seem to know everything about the missing link except the fact that it is missing."

Grant R. Jeffery said, "Darwin admitted that millions of 'missing links,' transitional life forms, would have to be discovered in the fossil record to prove the accuracy of his theory that all species had gradually evolved by chance mutation into new species. Unfortunately for his theory, despite hundreds of millions spent on searching for fossils worldwide for more than a century, the scientists have failed to locate *a single missing link* out of the millions that must exist if their theory of evolution is to be vindicated" (*The Signature of God*).

I can hardly believe that I once was a believer in such unfounded fables. The reason I approved of the idea was that it wasn't very important to me. As a Christian, however, the subject of origins now matters greatly to me because if evolution is true, the Bible is false. Modern evolutionary theory (as opposed to Darwin's original theory) says that man was once an ape. But the Bible says that there is one kind of flesh for man and another kind of flesh for animals (1 Corinthians 15:39). It also says that every animal reproduces "according to its kind." Dogs have puppies, not kittens. Cats have kittens, not chickens. Horses have foals, not calves. It doesn't matter how many thousands of years pass, elephants don't have giraffes, nor do monkeys have men.

It is interesting to note that pig heart valves have been used as replacements for human heart valves. Pig skin has even been grafted in humans to deal with severe burns. In fact, pig tissues are the nearest in chemical composition to those of humans. Perhaps wishful evolutionists should spend more time around the pigsty.

The "Big Bang" Theory

Try to think of any explosion that has produced order. Does a terrorist bomb create harmony? Big bangs cause chaos. How could a big bang produce a rose, apple trees, fish, sunsets, the seasons, humming birds, polar bears—thousands of birds and animals, each with its own eyes, nose, and mouth?

Here's an interesting experiment: Empty your garage of every piece of metal, wood, paint, rubber, and plastic. *Make sure nothing is there.* Nothing. Then wait for ten years and see if a Mercedes evolves. Try it. If it doesn't appear, leave it for 20 years. If that doesn't work, try it for 100 years. Then try leaving it for 10,000 years.

Here's what will produce the necessary blind faith to make the evolutionary process believable: leave it for 250 million years.

Professor Louis Bounoure, Director of Research, National Center of Scientific Research, so rightly stated: "Evolution is a fairy tale for grown-ups. This theory has helped nothing in the progress of science. It is useless."

The Bible tells us that animals are created "without understanding" (Psalm 32:9). Human beings are different from animals. We are made in God's "image." As human beings, we are aware of our "being." God is "I AM," and we know that "we are." We have understanding that we exist. We have a choice: to be, or not to be ... that is the question.

Among other unique characteristics, we have an innate ability to appreciate God's creation. What animal gazes with awe at a sunset, or at the magnificence of the Grand Canyon? What animal obtains joy from the sounds of music or takes the time to form itself into an orchestra to create music? We are also moral beings. What animal sets up court systems and apportions justice to its fellow creatures?

> IF EVOLUTION *IS* TRUE, THEN THE BIBLE IS NOT THE CREATOR'S REVELATION TO HUMANITY.

While birds and other creatures have instincts to create (nests, etc.), we have the ability to uncover the hidden laws of electricity. We can utilize the law of aerodynamics to transport ourselves around the globe. We also have the God-given ability to appreciate the value of creation. We unearth the hidden treasures of gold, silver, diamonds, and oil and make use of them for our own benefit. In addition, we have the unique ability to appreciate God for His incredible creation, and a spirit with which to respond to His love.

On February 3, 2002, *The [London] Observer* published an article that asked, "Is human evolution finally over?" According to one scientist, it is:

> "If you want to know what Utopia is like, just look around—this is it," said Professor Steve Jones of University College, London, who is to present his argu-

ment at a Royal Society Edinburgh debate, "Is Evolution Over?", next week. "Things have simply stopped getting better, or worse, for our species."

So that's it, folks. Mother Nature can't do anything to stop the thousands of diseases that plague humanity. While evolution carries on for all the animals, there will be no new lungs for those humans with emphysema and no new brains for those with brain disorders. The noses of those who live in Southern California will not evolve a smog filtration system, neither will orange pickers who have longer arms survive over the short-armed orange pickers. Men will not have their right hand evolve into a remote control, neither will drivers evolve hands-free cell phones on their chins. It seems that computer workers are stuck with repetitive motion disorders. With all the malfunctions of the human heart and desperate efforts by man to make artificial blood pumps, Mother Nature isn't going to help. It looks like she's stumped. She either doesn't know what to do, or she thinks that things are good enough. She started from nothing, made all this incredible creation, but for some reason she's not offering any improvements for the human race.

However, not all scientists agree with the theory that evolution has ended. One says that evolution is making our brains smaller, and, based on what they are telling us, I have to agree:

> Evolution goes on all the time. You don't have to intervene. It is just that it is highly unpredictable. For example, brain size has decreased over the past 10,000 years. A similar reduction has also affected our physiques. We are punier and smaller-brained compared with our ancestors only a few millennia ago. So even though we might be influenced by evolution, that does not automatically mean an improvement in our lot.

If evolution *is* true, then the Bible is not the Creator's revelation to humanity. On the negative side, this means that man has no ultimate purpose in life. On the positive side, it means neither is he ultimately responsible to any higher authority than what he places over himself. Therefore, "Let us eat, drink, and be merry, for tomorrow we die" would an appropriate life philosophy. You and I may embark upon any sinful pleasure our hearts desire, without any fear of retribution. This means we can ignore our consciences completely and sin with reckless abandon—clearly the erroneous philosophy of this generation.

Chapter Ten

WHO WROTE THE LETTER?

A FEW DAYS AFTER my conversion, I kept hearing my friend who had led me to Christ say, "Ray Comfort, a Christian?" He would shake his head and repeat the phrase. I was the last person in the world that he thought would want to become a Christian. I was so happy, I couldn't possibly be interested in everlasting life. *Little did he know.* I had everything I could ever want in this world, but I knew that time would rip it from my hands. My happiness-bubble was awaiting the sharp pin of reality.

The moment I was converted, the pin was dulled to a point of ineffectiveness. Suddenly, the Bible fascinated me. I read it with the fervor of a man gripped by gold fever. Was the Bible trustworthy? Could I believe what I read? Had it changed through the years, or was it full of mistakes, as is so often said?

When a man writes a letter, does *he* write it or does his *pen*? Obviously, he writes the letter, and the pen is the instrument he uses. The claim of the Bible is that it is God who did the writing, while men were the instruments He used to pen His letter to humanity (2 Peter 1:21). In 1947, the Dead Sea Scrolls were discovered. These manuscripts contained large portions of the Old Testament, a thousand years older than any other existing copies. Study of the scrolls has revealed that the Bible hasn't changed in content down through the ages as many skeptics had surmised. If the Bible is indeed the Word of our Creator, and it claims that our greatest enemy, death, has been destroyed, we would be fools not to at least give it a fleeting glance. But if it is merely a historical book, the writings of men, then it needs to be exposed as fraudulent because millions have been deceived by it.

The irony of the Christian faith is that it seems to be intellectual suicide, but proves to be the ultimate intellectual challenge.

In this chapter, we will look at numerous amazing scientific facts contained in Scripture. Keep in mind that the Bible was written by about forty men over a period of 1,600 years, beginning at 1500 B.C. If these men were inspired by God as the Bible claims, this should be no ordinary book. In light of these thoughts, let's look at the following.

- At a time when science taught that the earth sat on a foundation of either a large animal or a giant (1500 B.C), the Bible spoke of the earth's free float in space: "He hangs the earth on nothing" (Job 26:7).

- "Most cosmologists [scientists who study the origin and structure of the universe] agree that the Genesis account of creation, in imagining an initial void, may be uncannily close to the truth" (*Time*, December 1976).

- Science expresses the universe in five terms: time, space, matter, power, and motion. Genesis 1:1,2 revealed such truths to the Hebrews in 1450 B.C: "In the beginning [*time*] God created [*power*] the heaven [*space*] and the earth [*matter*] ... And the Spirit of God moved [*motion*] upon the face of the waters" (KJV). The very first thing God tells us is that He controls all aspects of the universe.

- The Bible also tells us that the earth is round: "It is He who sits above the circle of the earth" (Isaiah 40:22).

Secular man discovered this 2,400 years later.

- Not many people realize that radio waves and light waves are two forms of the same thing. God told this fact to Job in 1500 B.C: "Can you send out lightnings, that they may go, and say to you, 'Here we are!'?" (Job 38:35). Who would have believed that light could be sent and then manifest itself in speech? But did you know that radio waves travel at the speed of light? That's why you can have instantaneous wireless communication with someone on the other side of the earth. This was first realized in 1864 when "British scientist James Clerk Maxwell suggested that electricity and light waves were two forms of the same thing" (*Modern Century Illustrated Encyclopedia*).

- When science is in the dark about why the dinosaur[9] disappeared, the Bible would seem to shed light on the subject. In Job 40:15–24, God describes the largest of all the creatures He made. He speaks of this massive animal as being herbivorous (plant-eating), having its strength in its hips, a tail like a large tree, very strong bones, a habitat among the trees, able to consume large amounts of water, and being of great height. Then the Scriptures tell us, "Only He who made him can bring near His sword." In other words, God brought extinction to this huge creature.

- In Genesis 6, God gave Noah the dimensions of the 1.5 million cubic foot ark he was to build. In 1609 at Hoorn in Holland, a ship was built after that same pattern, revolutionizing shipbuilding. By 1900, every large ship on the high seas was inclined toward the proportions of the ark (as verified by "Lloyds Register of Shipping" in the *World Almanac*).

- Job stated that God "made a law for the rain, and a path for the thunderbolt" (Job 28:26). Centuries later, scientists began to discern the "law for the rain." Rainfall is part of a process called "the water cycle." The sun evaporates water from the ocean. The water vapor then rises and becomes clouds. This water in the clouds falls back to earth as rain, and collects in streams and rivers, then makes its way back to the ocean. That process repeats itself again and again. The idea of a complete water cycle was not fully understood until the seventeenth century. However, more than 2,000 years prior to the discoveries of Pierre Perrault, Edme Mariotte, and Edmund Halley, the Bible clearly described the hydrologic cycle.

  The Scriptures inform us, "If the clouds are full of rain, they empty themselves on the earth... All the rivers run into the sea, yet the sea is not full; to the place from which the rivers come, there they return again" (Ecclesiastes 11:3; 1:7). Amos 9:6 tells us that "He... calls for the waters of the sea, and pours them out on the face of the earth; the LORD is His name."

- Psalm 19:5,6 contains several interesting scientific facts. In speaking of the sun, the psalmist says that "its rising is from one end of heaven, and its circuit to the other end; and there is nothing hidden from its heat." For many years Bible critics scoffed at the Bible, citing that this verse taught the old false doctrine of geocentricity (i.e., the sun revolves around the earth). Then it was discovered in recent years that the sun is in fact moving through space. It is not stationary as was once thought. It is estimated to be moving at approximately 600,000 miles per hour, in an orbit so large that it would take approximately 200 million years to complete just one orbit.

- The Scriptures say, "Thus the heavens and the earth, and all the host of them, were finished" (Genesis 2:1). The Hebrew used the past definite tense for the verb "finished," indicating an action completed in the past, never again to occur. The creation was "finished"—once and for all. That is exactly what the First Law of Thermodynamics says. This law (often referred to as the Law of the Conservation of Energy and/or Mass) states that neither matter nor energy can be either created or destroyed. It was because of this Law that Sir Fred Hoyle's "Steady-State" (or "Continuous Creation") Theory was discarded. Hoyle stated that at points in the universe called *irtrons*, matter (or energy) was constantly being created. But the First Law states just the opposite. Indeed, there is no "creation" ongoing today. It is "finished" exactly as the Bible states.

- Three places in the Bible (Isaiah 5:6; Psalm 102:26; Hebrews 1:11) indicate that the earth is wearing out. This is what the Second Law of Thermodynamics (the Law of Increasing Entropy) states: that everything is running down and wearing out as energy is becoming less and less available for use. That means the universe will eventually "wear out" so much that (theoretically speaking) there will be a "heat death" and no more energy will be available for use. This wasn't discovered by man until fairly recently, but the Bible states it in clear, succinct terms.

- God told Abraham that on the eighth day newborn males were to be circumcised (Genesis 17:12). Why the eighth day? This is the day that the coagulating factor in the blood, called prothrombin, is the highest. Medical science has discovered that this is when the human body's immune system is at its peak.

- Genesis 3:15 reveals that a female possesses the "seed of life." This was not common knowledge until a few centuries ago. It was widely believed that only the male possessed the "seed of life" and that the woman was nothing more than an "incubator."

- Only in recent years has man discovered that there were mountains on the ocean floor. This was revealed in the Bible thousands of years ago. While deep in the ocean, Jonah cried, "I went down to the moorings of the mountains" (Jonah 2:6). The reason that the Bible and true science harmonize is that they have the same author.

- The Bible mentions "the fish of the sea that pass through the paths of the seas" (Psalm 8:8). Man discovered the existence of ocean currents in the 1850s, but the Bible declared the science of oceanography 2,800 years ago. Matthew Maury (1806–1873) is considered the father of oceanography. After noticing the expression "paths of the sea" in Psalm 8:8, Maury took God at His word and went looking for these paths. "If God said there are paths in the sea," Maury said, "I am going to find them." We are indebted to his discovery of the warm and cold continental currents. His book on oceanography, considered a foundational text on the subject, is still used in universities. Maury used the Bible as a guide to scientific discovery. If only more would use the Bible as a guide in their personal lives.

Many times I have heard the claim that the Bible is "full of mistakes." Over the years, I have spent thousands of hours searching the Scriptures, and I can't find one. There have been times when I thought I had found a mistake, but it was *my* mistake, not God's. I have often said that if anyone can prove to me that there is even one mistake in the Word of God, I will give them $1,000. Many people have tried to claim the cash, but they can never do it. This is because of the simple fact that "*all* Scripture is given by inspiration of God" (2 Timothy 3:16, emphasis added). *Everything* in the Bible is there because God put it there—so-called "mistakes" included. They are therefore not mistakes. In time, we will find that the "mistakes" are actually ours.

As Einstein said, "All our knowledge is but the knowledge of schoolchildren." There are many who, in a vain attempt to show atheism to be "intellectual," have claimed that Albert Einstein was an atheist. However, the father of all scientists made a number of statements that clearly refute such a claim. He said, "In the view of such harmony in the cosmos which I, with my limited human mind, am able to recognize, there are yet people who say there is no God. But what makes me really angry is that they quote me for support of such views." He also stated, "I want

> THE BIBLE IS NOT MERELY A HISTORY BOOK. IT IS ALSO A MORAL BOOK.

to know how God created this world. I am not interested in this or that phenomenon, in the spectrum of this or that element. I want to know His thoughts. The rest are details."

Those who take the time to read the Bible can know *how* God created this world (see Genesis chapter 1), and they can read the *thoughts of God* throughout His letter to humanity—holy Scripture. The problem is that the Bible is not merely a history book as some maintain. It is also a *moral* book, and for that reason sinful man refuses to open its pages. The psalmist informs us that "the entrance of Your words give light" (Psalm 119:130), and the Bible further tells us that men love darkness rather than light, because their deeds are evil. They refuse to come to the light because it exposes their sinful deeds (see John 3:19,20).

In light of these thoughts, it is interesting that at the reasonably young age of thirty-four Einstein unashamedly boasted, "I have firmly resolved to bite the dust, when my time comes, with the minimum of medical assistance, and up to then I will sin to my wicked heart's content." However, time tends to make most thinking men somewhat philosophical. Two months before his death in 1955, he said, "To one bent on age, death will come as a release. I feel this quite strongly now that I have grown old myself and have come to regard death like an old debt, at long last to be discharged. Still, instinctively one does everything possible to postpone the final settlement. Such is the game that Nature plays with us."[10]

It seems that the great genius spoke biblical truth unawares. However, it isn't Nature that seeks a "final settlement," it is the Law of God. Like a criminal who has transgressed civil law, Einstein (like the rest of humanity) was in debt to Eternal Justice because he had transgressed God's Law. This great debt that he spoke of could not be satisfied with mere silver and gold. It is a debt that demands capital punishment. It calls for the death penalty for guilty transgressors... and eternal damnation in hell. Its terrible decree demands, "The soul that sins shall die," but it is a demand that was fully satisfied but the One who cried from Calvary's cross, "It is finished!" It was paid in full by the precious blood of Jesus.

Chapter Eleven

BENEVOLENT JELLY

I T WAS AUGUST 1972. An antique Gestetner sat in my office. I didn't even know what a Gestetner was until that day. What looked like a legless lawn mower with a handle on one side was actually a hand-cranked copier. The Reverend George Densem, a ninety-one-year-old Presbyterian minister, had heard of my conversion and insisted on buying me one. He was adamant, and parted with his ninety dollars gladly.

A friend told me how to work the printing machine. It was just a matter of punching a stencil with a typewriter, placing the stencil over an ink-barrel, and turning the handle. I did as I was told, and, to my surprise, it worked—out the other end came a printed page.

My first evangelistic pamphlet was about racial problems in South Africa. From the time of my conversion, the issue concerned me. The whole world seemed intent on pointing a "holier than thou" finger at the sins of South Africa. I bounced off a hit song that went something like, "What we need is a great big melting pot—big enough to take the world and all it's got. Keep it stirring for a hundred years or more, and bring out coffee-colored people by the score." Even as a baby Christian I could see that the problem in South Africa wasn't skin color. If one segregates the whites from the blacks, there's still rape and murder. If one integrates the society, the skin color just sparks off the hatred that is already in the human heart. The heart of man is at the heart of man's problems. The Soviet leader of the sixties, Khrushchev, knew this. He said, "The chief failure with communism is its inability to create a new man." He was right. Communism says, "A new coat for every man," while Jesus Christ says, "A new man in every coat."

If I didn't like the way pigs lived, I could take a pig and scrub it clean, put deodorant under its pig-pits, and place it in a clean, thickly carpeted room. In a few days, however, the place would become a pigsty. The only way to change a pig is to change its nature. The same applies to man. Politics cannot change the heart of man. History proves that. The only One who can change the human heart is Almighty God. When the appliance breaks down, take a look at the Instruction Book. The Bible says that sin is the cause of all human suffering; Jesus Christ is the only cure.

THE BIBLE SAYS THAT SIN IS THE CAUSE OF ALL HUMAN SUFFERING; JESUS IS THE ONLY CURE.

That was the message of my first tract. Another Christian saw it and ordered 5,000 copies, much to the dismay of my right arm. It wasn't long before I sold the man-handled lawn mower and used a more modern means to print tracts, which, thanks to God, have run into the millions. It seems as fast as our ministry has grown, so has man's ability to blame the symptoms rather than the cause. Not only does he think that the problem is skin (rather than sin), he insists on making statements like, "Money is the root of all evil," when it's not. The Bible says, "The *love of money* is a root of all kinds of evil" (1 Timothy 6:10, emphasis added). Man prefers to pass the buck when the buck is his. How can money be evil? It is his *greed* that is evil.

America doesn't have a *drug* problem; it has a *people* problem. It is people that abuse drugs. Rarely does man say the problem is with man himself. He will always blame someone else. I know, because I did three-and-a-half years of hard labor (as a pastor), listening to husbands blame wives and wives blame husbands. If it's not someone else's fault, then it must be God's fault. When God caught Adam in his rebellion, Adam blamed "the woman whom You gave to be with me" (Genesis 3:12). It was either the woman, or it was God, but it wasn't Adam who was at fault. A godly person will always justify God, while a guilty person will always try to justify himself. Even insurance companies do the same. When they have a disaster and no one to blame, they call it "an act of God."

Let Sleeping Dogs Lie

Consider the way dogs cross the road. The dog will blindly wander onto a freeway oblivious to the danger. His tail wags as he steps between cars without a second thought. Cars swerve. Tires squeal. The noise is deafening as vehicles smash into each other. The sleepy dog stops wagging his tail for a moment and looks at the pile of smoldering, broken cars on the freeway. His expression betrays his thoughts. His bone-burying brain doesn't realize for one moment that he is responsible for the disaster.

When man wanders onto the freeway of sin, his tail wags with delight. He thinks that this was what he was made for. His thoughts of any repercussions for his actions are shallow. His mind wanders into lust, and then predictably he wanders onto the path of adultery. Suddenly a disaster sits before him. His marriage is shattered, his name is slurred, his children are twisted and scarred. But like the dumb dog, he doesn't realize for one moment that he is solely responsible for his sin. As far as he is concerned, he had good reason to do what he did.

Perhaps you do see that you are to blame. Perhaps you know that you have sinned, but you have genuine difficulties with Christianity. Maybe you are "almost persuaded to become a Christian." It could be that you are biblically misinformed due to books you have read or what you have been told. Whatever the case, let's look at some of the most common objections to the Christian faith and see if we can clear them from your vision.

First, let's pry into the private life of one of our ancestors. It seems that the entire non-Christian world wants to know the details of where Cain got his wife.[11] I will resist the temptation to say, "I would tell you if I was Abel." Cain simply married a distant sister. God told Adam and Eve to be fruitful and multiply. That doesn't mean that they were to get into gardening and math. They were commanded by God to have children. No doubt they joyfully obeyed. We don't know how long it was until Cain took a wife, but if you put two rabbits together (male and female), even if you don't encourage them to mate, you will have a plague of rabbits before you know it. Those who are quick to say that Cain committed incest should realize that when there is no law, there is no transgression. But as the population grew large enough, and as the risk of genetic problems increased because of sin's curse, God outlawed marriage between siblings.

Maybe you've thought, "You can't tell me that a loving God will send innocent aborigines to hell merely because they don't believe in Jesus." I agree with you. God won't send innocent natives to hell merely because they don't believe in Him. They will go to hell for murder, rape, lust, pride, hatred, lying, stealing, kidnapping, cannibalism, anger, deceit, torture, greed, adultery, etc. God doesn't overlook sin because of skin color or geographic location. The only covering for sin is the blood of Jesus Christ.

Your next thought may be, "So you're saying that those who repent and trust in Jesus will be saved, and those who can't, because they haven't heard the gospel, will go to hell?" On Judgment Day, God will do what is right. The Bible says, "And how shall they believe in Him of whom they have not heard? And how shall they hear without a preacher?" (Romans 10:14). If you really care for the heathen, get right with God yourself, and then take them the good news of the forgiveness in Christ. Or is it closer to the truth that you couldn't care less about "innocent aborigines," and all you really want is to find an excuse to hold on to your sins?

What about all the suffering in the world? Surely that's evidence that the Bible is wrong in saying that God is love. God is not just one great big piece of benevolent jelly. He is not smiling at the human race. In fact, the Bible says that He is full of fury. The day is coming when He will "render His anger with fury, and His rebuke with flames of fire" (Isaiah 66:15). There are a few things in this area that I don't understand, but the day will come when I will understand all things. In the meantime, I will trust God and use the understanding I do have. What I do understand is this: The Scriptures tell us that God's "judgments are in all the earth"—that He holds back rain, sends lightning, and causes earthquakes. I don't know how many of the estimated one million earthquakes each year are merely workings of nature or are actual judgments of God.

A little boy once said to his mom, "I am sick of the food you keep giving me—potatoes, carrots, and spinach. From now on I choose my own diet. I am having nothing but chocolate candy bars for breakfast, lunch, and dinner." Imagine what the child would look like if he were allowed to eat what he wanted. He may become very sick and even die because of a lack of proper nutrition. His face would break into pimples, giving evidence that he is on the wrong diet—even though it tastes good *to* him; it's not good *for* him.

Man's attitude is, "God, from now on, I don't want your diet—I want mine." He chooses sin rather than righteousness. He wants what *tastes* good rather than what *is* good. As a direct result of humanity's sinful diet, painful pimples have broken out over the whole face of the earth. There are diseases, floods, earthquakes, starvation, endless suffering, and death. All these things should show us that something is radically wrong with our diet. Instead of using the sufferings of humanity as an excuse to reject God, see them as stark evidences to accept Him and the explanations given in His Word. They are very real reminders that what God says is true. If we throw out the pilot because we want to take over the controls, we shouldn't moan when the plane heads for disaster.

> MAN WANTS WHAT *TASTES* GOOD RATHER THAN WHAT *IS* GOOD.

Chapter Twelve

THE REAL THING

PERHAPS THE greatest hindrance to people coming to Christ is the blatant hypocrisy within Christianity. Maybe your argument goes like this: "The Church is full of hypocrites, and besides, nothing has caused more wars in history than religion." No argument there. But let's take a look at what a hypocrite is. The word means "pretender." In other words, the hypocrite is not a Christian, he is pretending. He is a non-Christian who is pretending to be a Christian. He's not on our side, he's on yours.

The way bank employees learn to recognize counterfeit bills is to study the genuine article. When they see the false, they spot it because their eye is trained to know the real thing. The real thing in Christianity is someone who is faithful, kind, loving, good, gentle, humble, patient, and self-controlled, and who will speak the truth in love. So the next time you're watching TV, and see a black-hatted, Abraham Lincoln–style bearded, booze-sodden, Old-English speaking, Bible-quoting hypocrite plunge a pitchfork into his neighbor's back "in the name of the Lord," ask yourself, "Is this a genuine Christian? Does he love his neighbor as himself? Is he kind, gentle, good, generous, and self-controlled? Does he love his enemies? Does he do good to those who spitefully use him?" If not, then you have another non-Christian who is pretending to be a Christian. Nothing new there. Non-Christians caused the First and Second World Wars, the Korean War, the Vietnam War, and what's worse, they're still causing wars in the name of God. When the Falkland Islands crisis broke out the British said, "God is with us." So did the Argentines. Americans are well-versed in "Praise the Lord, and pass the ammunition." The Nazis had "*Got mitt uns*" (God with us) engraved on their belt buckles.

No, one doesn't have to go to church to see the hypocrite. In fact, the best place to look for the hypocrite is in the mirror. Who of us can claim to be always free from pretense? The hypocrite is the teenager who is pure in front of his parents, but burns with lust in his heart. The hypocrite is the businessman who is smooth and polished and signs his letters "Yours sincerely," but cuts his client's throat for a fast buck. The hypocrite acts like a virtuous spouse, but feasts her covetous heart on the adulteries of soap operas. Hypocrisy is having "In God we trust" on our money, when it is nothing but a pretense. Hypocrites sing "God Bless America," yet use His holy name to curse.

> ONE DOESN'T HAVE TO GO TO CHURCH TO SEE THE HYPOCRITE.

Hypocrites are those whose Pilgrim fathers established "one nation under God," but give homage to a stone idol, a goddess of liberty, spending millions on a face-lift, saying, "She is a light to the world; she has given us freedom." Hypocrisy is the pretense of concern for the health of cigarette smokers, warning of the fatal effects of tobacco, but reaping $32 billion in revenue each year from the deadly drug. Hundreds of thousands of Americans die annually as a direct result of cigarette smoking. Hypocrisy is a society that says it cares for children, yet murders millions in the womb. The hypocrite can see sin in South Africa, but never in himself. If the whole world hates the hypocrite, what must God think of him? All hypocrites will go to hell. If the hypocrite so offends you, you won't want to spend eternity in hell with him, will you?

If your whole life (including your secret thoughts and deeds) were made public, would you be free of pretense in the sight of the world? If the press of America had access to your every secret, could you run for political office, or would you find yourself in the tabloid headlines?

We need to be careful when we judge others. We can often make tragic errors when we come to a quick conclusion that someone is a hypocrite. If we don't have the truth, the whole truth, and nothing but the truth, we can judge someone as being guilty when he is innocent. There is only One who has total truth about each of us, and His judgment is and will be "according to righteousness."

An atheist may think it adds to his credibility to say that he was once a Christian, but that he realized Christianity was a myth and turned from the faith. His admission places him in a dilemma in which there are only two alternatives: 1) He "knew the Lord" (see Jeremiah 9:23,24; John 17:3), thereby admitting that God is real; or 2) He *thought* he knew the Lord, but he (in his words) "was deceived." He, then, is admitting that he didn't know the Lord, and was therefore never a Christian but merely a pretender.

Knock, Knock

We were once plagued by a large spider web on the side of our home. It didn't matter how many times I got rid of it, the next morning there was a brand new one. The problem was that I could not find the spider.

One day, armed with a small stick in one hand and repellent in the other, I crept up to the web and gently tapped it with the stick. I could almost hear the spider stirring from sleep and mumbling, "Good—breakfast!" With Daniel, my youngest son, cleverly imitating the sound of a distressed pre-breakfast fly, the spider didn't stand a chance. He sprung from his hiding place and rushed into the middle of his web. For a split second, he looked like a soldier caught in a surprise attack of the enemy. Then, before he could retreat, I blasted him (without mercy) with the repellent. Instead of dealing with the symptom, I had gone for the cause.

Check the television news or your daily newspaper and you will see that the tangled webs of deceit, hatred, divorce, wife-beating, child molestation, murder, greed, rape, assaults, incest, kidnapping, lust, adultery, terrorism, envy, etc., are spun across the whole earth. But where is the spider? He sleeps quietly, unseen by the human eye. How do we then bring him into the light? The answer is the stick of God's Law. It is the only means of revealing him. If we open up the Moral Law, it will cause his ugly head to appear.

Later, if you are willing, we will lure him out into the open and with the help of God, spray him with the "gospel spray" of the blood of Jesus Christ.

Chapter Thirteen

DEATH SENTENCE FOR ERROR

T HE BIBLE states that if a prophet was not one hundred percent accurate in his prophecy, he was to be put to death. If the Bible is the Book of the Creator, its prophecies will be perfectly accurate. Bear in mind the faultless description the Bible gives of this day and age in which we live (the "latter days"), as we look at the "signs of the times." These signs are to warn us of the coming day when Almighty God reveals Himself to humanity, when His kingdom comes to earth, and His will is done on earth "as it is in heaven."

- False Bible teachers will be money hungry, smooth talkers, have many followers, and will slur the Christian faith (2 Peter 2:1–3).

- Earthquakes will be widespread (Matthew 24:7). Science estimates that there are a million earthquakes each year, with up to twenty occurring at any given moment.

- Many wars will erupt (Matthew 24:6). There have been over one hundred wars since 1945, with more than 16 million deaths.

- Deadly diseases will be prevalent (Matthew 24:7). According to the American Cancer Society, each year "about 552,200 Americans are expected to die of cancer, more than 1,500 people a day. Cancer is the second leading cause of death in the U.S., exceeded only by heart disease. In the U.S., one of four deaths is from cancer. Nearly five million lives have been lost to cancer since 1990." An estimated 16.3 million people have died from AIDS since the epidemic began; 12.7 million were adults (including 6.2 million women), and 3.6 million were children under 15.

- People will forsake the Ten Commandments as a moral code (lawlessness), committing adultery, stealing, lying, and killing (Matthew 24:12). Recently there were 2,300 murders in one year in Los Angeles.

- There will be a cold religious system denying God's power (2 Timothy 3:5).

- The Bible warns that these times will reveal a great increase in the occult (1 Timothy 4:1). A look at television or newspapers will show how prevalent it is in society. In the U.S. alone, there are 10,000 full-time and 175,000 part-time astrologers.

- Men will substitute fables in place of Christian truth (2 Timothy 4:4). This is so evident at Christmas when the birth of the Savior is lost behind the myth of Santa Claus. It is also seen in the faddish New Age religions.

- The fact that God once flooded the earth (the Flood of Noah) will be denied (2 Peter 3:5).

- There will be an increase in famines (Matthew 24:7).

- The institution of marriage will be forsaken (1 Timothy 4:3).

- Interest in vegetarianism will increase (1 Timothy 4:3).

- There will be hypocrites in the church (Matthew 23:25–30).

- There will be an increase in religious cults (Matthew 24:11).

- There will be much intimidation from nation to nation (Matthew 24:7).

- Humanity will become very materialistic (2 Timothy 3:5).

- The Christian gospel will be preached as a warning to all nations (Matthew 24:14).

- Christians will be hated (Luke 21:17).

- Many who profess to be Christians will fall away from their faith (Matthew 24:10).

- There will be an increase in pestilence. In the United States, 390,000 tons of pesticides are sprayed on crops each year to prevent the growing problem (*U.S. News and World Report*, November 16, 1987).

- Youth will become rebellious (2 Timothy 3:2).

- Men will mock the signs of the end of the age by saying, "These signs have always been around." This will be because they fail to understand that God is not subject to the dimension of time (2 Peter 3:4).

- The sign that is the culmination of all these signs will be the Israeli occupation of Jerusalem (Luke 21:29,30). In 1948, after over 1,900 years without a homeland, the Jews set foot in Jerusalem, fulfilling these words of Jesus Christ that were spoken 2,000 years earlier. God had warned that if the Jews forsook His Law, He would scatter them throughout the earth, allowing them to be put to shame. Then He would draw them back to Israel (Ezekiel 36:24). In Isaiah 66:8 (700 B.C.), Isaiah prophesied: "Shall the earth be made to give birth in one day? Or shall a nation be born at once? For as soon as Zion was in labor, she gave birth to her children." In 1922, the League of Nations gave Great Britain the mandate (political authority) over Palestine. On May 14, 1948, Britain withdrew her mandate, and the nation of Israel was "born in a day."

There are more than twenty-five Bible prophecies concerning Palestine that have been literally fulfilled. The probability of these being accidentally fulfilled are slightly more than one chance in 33,000,000. The nation of Israel is the night-light on the clock of Bible prophecy. Its occupation of Jerusalem shows us how close we are to the "midnight hour." Scripture also informs us that Jerusalem will become a "burdensome stone for all people" (Zechariah 12:3).

- In Genesis, the book of beginnings, God said that Ishmael (the progenitor of the Arab race—see *Time*, April 4, 1988) would be a "wild man; his hand shall be against every man, and every man's hand against him. And he shall dwell in the presence of all his brethren" (Genesis 16:12). Four thousand years later, who could deny that this prophecy is being fulfilled in the Arab race? The Arabs and the Jews are "brethren," having the same ancestors. The whole Middle East conflict is caused by their dwelling together.

Russia and Israel

A number of books of the Bible speak of events that are still in the future. Ezekiel 38 (written approximately 600 B.C.) prophesies that in these times ("the latter days," verse 16), Russia (referred to as the "Prince of Rosh," *Smith's Bible Dictionary*) will combine with Iran, Libya (in Hebrew called "Put"), and communistic Ethiopia (in Hebrew called "Cush") and attack Israel (verses 5-8). This will take place after an Israeli peace initiative has been successful (verse 11). The Bible even gives the Russian reasoning for and the direction of the attack (verses 10–15) as well as the location of the battle (Armageddon—Revelation 16:16). This is generally interpreted as meaning "the mountain of Megiddo," which is located on the north side of the plains of Jezreel. Russia has had a foothold in the Middle East for many years: "The Soviets are entrenched around the rim of the Middle East heartland, in Afghanistan, South Yemen, Ethiopia, and Libya" ("Countdown in the Middle East," *Reader's Digest*, May 1982).

ISRAEL IS THE NIGHT-LIGHT ON THE CLOCK OF BIBLE PROPHECY.

It would seem from the Scriptures that nuclear weapons will be used in this battle. The Bible speaks of search parties looking for bones of those killed in the war. When a bone is located, it will not be touched. A "marker" will be set by it, and it will be buried by special teams (Ezekiel 39:14,15), more than likely a reference to radioactive contamination. The Book of Joel (800 B.C.) also speaks of this war. It seems to confirm the nuclear weapon aspect with "pillars of smoke" being seen during the battle (Joel 2:30). It also seems that there will be flame-throwing tank warfare. Not having a word for "tank," the prophet describes his vision of these war machines with the following: "A fire devours before them,...they climb the wall...; every one marches in formation,...they run to and fro in the city, they run on the wall;...the earth quakes before them" (Joel 2:3–10). Back in 1988, Russia had 41,000 tanks.

Israel will never have lasting peace until she obeys God.

If she will obey His statutes and keep His commandments, He will give her rain in due season, an abundance of food, freedom from fear, victory over the enemy, and peace within the land (Leviticus 26:1–13). Sadly, from what we see of the Scriptures, Israel will seek God only as a last resort, when she sees that she cannot prevail against the might and power of the Russian invasion (Joel 2:12–20). Deuteronomy 4:30 warns that it will take tribulation to turn Israel to God in the latter days. When Israel finally turns to God in true repentance, He will take pity on His people and remove far from them the "northern army" (Joel 2:20).

Another sign of the latter days will be a clear understanding of the judgments and the will of God. No other generation has seen what we are seeing take place in the Middle East. No other generation has had the scientific knowledge to help it understand "strange" Scriptures, that made no sense until scientific discoveries showed them to be true. Nor has any other generation had access to the Bible as we have. We can understand perfectly the times in which we live: "The anger of the LORD will not turn back until He has executed and performed the thoughts of His heart. In the latter days you will understand it perfectly" (Jeremiah 23:20). Keep one eye on the Middle East—and the other toward the heavens.

Chapter Fourteen

BIZARRE TO THE INSANE

A TELEVISION NEWS reporter stated, "Tonight we will look at the buying and selling of the world's most priceless commodity: information." He was right. Information is the world's most priceless commodity. If you have information about where oil deposits are, or about the location of gold or diamonds in the earth, you can be a billionaire overnight. Information can even save your life. If you are in a burning building and you know the location of the fire escapes, you can find your way out. If you are without that information, you will probably die. It is not just having the information that matters, it's what you *do* with that information that counts. The information must govern your actions.

A man in the U.S. once wanted to paint his steep A-frame roof. Because his ladder was too short to reach the top, he threw a heavy rope over the roof, went around to the front, and carefully secured the rope to the back of his car. He then went to the back of the house, climbed up onto his roof with the rope tied firmly around his waist, and began painting.

His wife, not knowing what he had done, came out of the house with car keys in hand, got into the car and drove off. He was pulled over the top of the roof and was seriously injured.

Perhaps you see nothing wrong with believing the theory of evolution, even if it can't be substantiated. But remember —your information will govern your actions. If you believe a drink contains poison, you won't drink it. If you believe it is safe, you will drink it. If you believe evolution is true, and from that premise believe that the Bible is false, then you won't repent. Like the man who secured himself to the car, you will find that you are only as secure as the object to which you have secured yourself. If your faith is placed in evolution and not in God's promises, you will find that the object to which you have tied yourself will be your eternal downfall. You will perish because you refused information that would have saved your most prized possession—your soul.

Cozy Cocoon

I once watched a documentary that had me glued to the television screen. The program was about a man who played castanets to his tomatoes. The subject moved from the bizarre to the insane when the gentleman placed earphones on his tomatoes and played classical music to them—in stereo, of course. This man was a nut.

I was about to turn the TV off in disgust when I heard something that radically changed my mind. The man's name was in *The Guinness Book of World Records* for having the world's largest tomato: four-and-a-half pounds! I learned a valuable lesson that day—never knock something until you see its results.

The next time you see a caterpillar on a leaf, study it for a while. You will notice that it twists and turns until it has wound itself into a web, finally encasing itself in a cocoon. We don't knock what it's doing because we know a metamorphosis is taking place within the cocoon. A miracle of nature is happening. In time, a beautiful butterfly will appear.

To those who don't understand, Christians are doing no more than wrapping themselves with rules and regulations, hiding from the real world in the cocoon of Christianity. But wait—don't knock it until you see the results. When you look at the Church today, you're looking at the grub. Granted, we do seem to lack in so many areas. But the same One who created the process of metamorphosis is all the while at work in the hearts of those who love Him, and the day will come when the butterfly will emerge.

Light Relief

This may seem unthinkable, but just imagine that the Bible, Jesus Christ, and Almighty God, the Creator of the universe, are right and you are wrong. Imagine that. *You being wrong?* Look at it this way. If you are right and there is no Creator, no afterlife, no justice, no heaven and no hell, you won't even get the chance to say, "I told you so!" If you are right, then creation was an accident, the Bible is nothing but fables, Jesus Christ was a liar, Christians are deceived, and I have spent hours pouring out my heart into this book for nothing.

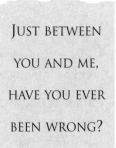

JUST BETWEEN YOU AND ME, HAVE YOU EVER BEEN WRONG?

But if what I am saying is true, the atheist will get the shock of his life—at his death. He will wake up dead, and will find that he truly has "passed on." I ask again, is it possible that you could be wrong? Come on, bend a little. Just between you and me, have you ever been wrong? Are you divinely infallible? Are you different from the rest of us? Human nature is prone to error; the person who invented the pencil eraser knew that.

To make the point—and for a little light relief—I submit the following evidence of human error. I don't do this in condescension, because I know that none of us is inflammable (oops—infallible). We *all* make mistakes.

These are actual statements taken from applications for

support received by a large city's welfare department:

- I am forwarding my marriage certificate and six children. I have seven, but one died which was baptized on a half sheet of paper.

- I am writing the Welfare Department to say that my baby was born two years old. When do I get my money?

- You have changed my little boy to a girl. Will this make a difference?

- I cannot get sick pay. I have six children. Can you tell me why?

- I am glad to report that my husband who is missing is dead.

- This is my eighth child. What are you going to do about it?

- Please find for certain if my husband is dead. The man I am now living with can't eat or do anything till he knows.

- I am very much annoyed to find you have branded my son illiterate. This is a dirty lie as I was married a week before he was born.

- In answer to your letter, I have given birth to a boy weighing ten pounds. I hope this is satisfactory.

- I am forwarding my marriage certificate and three children one of which is a mistake as you can see.

- Unless I get my husband's money pretty soon, I will be forced to live an immortal life.

- In accordance with your instructions I have given birth to twins in the enclosed envelope.

Chapter Fifteen

GOING FOR THE SPIDER

IT'S BEEN SAID that the worst thing you can ever tell a person is, "You are wrong." It is a sad indictment on humanity that the statement is probably true. Even if someone is completely in the wrong and you tell him so without discretion, you will more than likely alienate yourself from him. Being wrong is a blow to the proud human ego.

You may have picked up this book totally convinced that there was no proof that God existed. But as you read its pages, you began to see that there is another point of view. Perhaps you have become convinced that God is a reality, and that the Bible is indeed the Word of God. It is my hope that this revelation has come to you in a spirit of gentleness on my part, so that you won't feel alienated from me, because I want to speak from my heart to yours.

Imagine we are seated next to each other in a plane. I have very reliable information that we are about to crash. In fact, the whole aircraft is rocking and shaking so much that it seems it may fall to pieces at any moment. Still, I'm not too fearful, because I've reached under my seat, found a parachute, and put it on. What concerns me is that you don't see the need to put yours on. Even though you know you have to jump, you have three lines of argument about why you should leave the parachute off. First, you're adamant that the plane had no maker. Second, you have noticed that a number of the other passengers say they're wearing a parachute when it's obvious to you that they are not. Third, you think that you can somehow defy the law of gravity.

I feel a little embarrassed at having to point out to you that if the plane was made, there must be a maker. But after a while you see my reasoning. You also accept my answer to your second objection—that if the other passengers want to pretend they were wearing a parachute, they will find out their mistake when they jump. My suggestion to you is to put yours on first, then see if you can persuade the "pretenders" to put theirs on.

The third objection is also answered by simple logic. I found that the most effective way to convince you of your need is to hang you out the door of the plane by your ankles. I don't do this literally. I merely talk about what happens to a human body when it impacts the ground at 120 mph. You finally realize your need to put the parachute on. I feel at peace about having you put it on for a motive of self-preservation.

The Main Objections

Let's now swing from this allegory to real life. We will say that your two main objections about why you shouldn't accept the Savior were the question of God's existence and the fact of hypocrisy in the Church. However, you have become convinced of God's reality, and you accept that He will judge hypocrites. When they die, they will see their error.

Your problem now is that you still think you don't need a Savior. You don't believe you need someone to stand on your behalf as an advocate for your defense before the Judge of the universe. You think that you can somehow defy the Moral Law of God.

Please, trust me for a moment while I attempt to hang you out the door of the plane by your ankles. It will be a fearful experience, but it is most necessary. It should have the effect of helping you to see the seriousness of what I am trying to say.

My aim is not to convince you of the existence of the Moral Law. You already know it exists. The Bible says that the "work of the law" is written in your heart, and that your conscience bears witness (Romans 2:15). God has given light to every man. You have always known that it is wrong to kill, to steal, to lie, to commit adultery, etc. You have even known in your heart that God exists. Michael Pearl rightly said, "When a man calls himself an atheist, he is not attacking God; he is attacking his own conscience." Your conscience has always been there as a judge in the courtroom of your mind. It has given you the knowledge of what is right and wrong. My aim is rather to persuade you of the *consequences* of breaking that Law. All I require is to get a good grip on the ankles of your honesty.

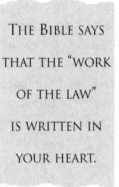

THE BIBLE SAYS THAT THE "WORK OF THE LAW" IS WRITTEN IN YOUR HEART.

To do this, we will thoroughly go through the Ten Commandments to see if you have broken any of them. As we do so, remember these three facts:

- God sees the sins of your youth as though it were yesterday. Just as time doesn't forgive transgression of civil law (i.e., a murderer is still a murderer ten years after the crime), so time doesn't forgive sin.

- God sees your thought-life. He made the mind of man, so surely He can see what he made. Nothing is hidden from His omniscient eye.

- He is perfect, just, good, holy, and utterly righteous. By

His very nature, He must punish transgression of His Law. If He sees a murder take place, He must eventually bring the murderer to justice. This is something that the most dimwitted of us can understand, even if there is disagreement on the form of punishment.

The Law

It is important to realize that being a Christian doesn't determine that you will exist eternally. It just defines the location. We will all exist forever. A great preacher once said, "Death is not the termination of existence. It is the entrance into an eternal, unchanging state." If you die in your sins, God will judge you accordingly. There is no allowance in the Scriptures for "purgatory," no place for a second chance.

The Bible reveals that each of us has failed to put God first. We have failed to love Him with our heart, mind, soul and strength. It states plainly, "There is none who understands; there is none who seeks after God" (Romans 3:11). *The First Commandment* is to put God first in our affections. That's not an option. It's a command.

Imagine buying a toy for a child's pleasure and having him love the toy more than he loves you. Yet, isn't that what you've done with God? Didn't He shower the gift of life upon you, giving you freedom, food, family, eyes, ears, and a mind with which to think? Yet you have used that mind to deny the existence of the One who gave you the mind in the first place.

Isn't it true that you have been guilty of ingratitude? If someone gave you a car as a gift, should you thank the person? Have you ever humbly thanked God for the gift of life? If you have, but you've never obeyed His command to repent of your sins, then your "thanks" is nothing but empty words.

If you love anything more than you love God—your

spouse, sibling, career, car, sports, or even your own life—you are loving the gift more than the Giver. What do you have that you didn't receive? Everything you have came to you through the goodness of God. Jesus said that we should so love God that all our other affections—for mother, father, brother, sister, and our own life—should seem like "hate" compared to the love we have for the God who gave those loved ones and that life to us. It has been rightly said that if the Greatest Commandment is to love God with all of our heart, mind, soul, and strength, then the greatest sin is failure to do so.

The Bible also says that the First Commandment involves loving your neighbor as yourself. Are you familiar with what is commonly called the "good Samaritan"? The man picked up a beaten stranger, tended to his wounds, and carried him to an inn. He then gave money for his care and told the innkeeper that he would cover all the man's expenses. That's a picture of how God *commands* us to treat our fellow human beings. We should love them as much as we love ourselves—whether they are friend or foe. In fact, Jesus didn't call the helper in that story the "good" Samaritan. He wasn't good. He merely carried out the basic requirements of the Law. Have you loved humanity as yourself? You be the judge. Have you kept the Law? It will be the standard of God's judgment on the Day of Wrath. Will you be innocent or guilty on Judgment Day? I'm not judging you; I'm asking you to judge yourself. The sentence for a transgression of the First Commandment is death.

The Second Commandment is, "You shall not make for yourself a carved image." (You won't find this Commandment in the traditional Roman Catholic teaching. It was removed because it exposed idolatry within the church—bowing down to statues. They deleted it and split the Tenth Commandment into two in order to bring the total back to ten Commandments.) This command means that we shouldn't make a god in our own image, either with our hands or with our minds. I was guilty of this. I made a god to suit myself. My god didn't mind lust, and a fib here or there. He didn't have *any* moral dictates. In truth, my god didn't exist. He was a figment of my imagination, shaped to conform to my sins. Almost all unsaved people have an idolatrous understanding of the nature of God.

Let me show you what I mean. Although the Bible says that humanity hates God without cause, most would deny that fact. You may not hate your god, but look at the biblical revelation of our Creator. God killed a man because He didn't like his sexual activities. He commanded Joshua to kill every Canaanite man, woman, and child, without mercy. He drowned the whole human race, except for Noah and his family, in the Flood. He killed a man for merely touching the Ark of the Covenant. In the New Testament, He killed a husband and wife because they told one lie. That God, says humanity, is not so easy to snuggle up against.

> MY GOD WAS A FIGMENT OF MY IMAGINATION, SHAPED TO CONFORM TO MY SINS.

Before you ask why God killed a couple for telling a lie, ask, "Why didn't God kill me, when I lied for the first time?" God simply treated them according to their sins. When we did wrong for the first time and didn't get struck by lightning, we then concluded that God didn't see or didn't care about what we did. With that, we became bolder in our sin.

If we caught a true revelation of God, we would fall flat on our faces in terror. Take an objective look at some of His natural laws. If you break electrical or gravitational laws, the consequences are fearful. But they are merely a pale shadow of the eternal Moral Law of God. My feeble words cannot express what God is like, but His Law gives us some insight into His holy nature. The Law reveals utter holiness, supreme righteousness, and absolute truth. God has a violent passion for justice.

What has your understanding of God been like? Do you tremble at the very thought of His power and holiness? Have you seen Him in the light of the Holy Scriptures, or have you made up a god to suit yourself? If the latter, then you are guilty of "idolatry." The Law's sentence for idolatry is death, and, according to the Scriptures, no idolater will enter the kingdom of heaven.

The Third Commandment is, "You shall not take the name of the LORD your God in vain."

I wonder if you have ever given any thought to the origin of cursing. It's rather strange. The words used to curse may be quite an inoffensive part of the English language. Take for instance "damn" and "hell." The words in themselves have legitimate meanings. However, the manner in which they are used determines whether they fit the category of curse words.

Let's look at a few common words in the vernacular, and see if we can understand how they made it onto the pop chart of cursing. First, the ever-popular curse word (a word often used in Scripture): "bastard." In recent years, many have looked at wedlock and concluded that anything ending with "lock" is a little too binding. So they have chosen to keep the door open and live with someone, without the vows of marriage. Consequently, many of today's children are in essence "bastards"—they are born out of wedlock. Yet, despite the fact that illegitimacy no longer carries the social stigma it once had, the word itself still carries strong connotations. To call someone by that word still packs a powerful punch and makes it number one on the insult/cursing charts.

This brings us to the second category, that of "circumstantial cursing." Take Joe Average. Joe had a very restless night's sleep. He tossed and turned until the early hours of the morning, finally drifting off around five o'clock. After being awakened by his alarm at six, he felt worse than he did before he went to sleep. He burned his breakfast toast, the coffee in the microwave boiled over, and as he got in his car, he felt very close to the boiling point himself. Never mind, at least he wasn't late for work. He had set his alarm to go off a little earlier than usual because he had arrived ten minutes late for work the previous day. His boss had given him such a dressing down that he wanted to be early today. Upsetting the boss had been the reason for such a sleepless night.

Joe sat in his car, paused for a moment, and took a deep breath to try to release his frustrations. As he reached out and turned the key in the ignition, he sat in stunned disbelief. The battery gave a last pathetic and dying grunt. Joe's eyes burned with rage. He grasped the steering wheel with an iron grip, and breathed out through gritted teeth the internationally, ever-popular curse word beginning with "s." He wanted to express utter disgust, and the word seemed to fit the situation as far as he was concerned.

The reason for using these words to curse a person or a situation is reasonably obvious. However, the purpose in using what, in respectable circles, is commonly called the "f" word is a little more obscure. (I hope such talk doesn't offend you. I am trying to be discreet because I want to make an important point.) Most are aware that the word is slang to describe physical intimacy between a husband and wife. Using the word as an insult/curse may arise from the fact that many years ago a person caught in unlawful sex was punished by being sent to the stocks. Their crime was said to be "For Unlawful Carnal Knowledge." The words have evolved over the years to mean more than they were originally intended. To express the desire for a fellow human being to be in such a state has grown to become a gross insult. In fact, the term is still so offensive that it may even get you arrested if you use it in a public place.

Despite the fact that Joe Average arrived twenty minutes late for work, he kept his job. But the look his boss had given him was worse than the verbal dressing down he had the day before. Joe knew he was skating on thin ice.

Not Even a Groan

Insomnia seemed to come in waves with Joe. Once again he had tossed and turned for what seemed like an eternity, before getting a few hours of sleep. But this day, he was determined to make it to work on time. He needed to hang on to this job. To ensure this, he put a new battery in the car and set his alarm clock to go off even earlier. He wanted everything to run more smoothly today. He even stood over the toaster to make sure the toast didn't burn. Making it to the other side of breakfast without mishap, though, didn't seem to help his disposition one bit. Lack of sleep made him feel like a crystal vase waiting to be shattered.

As he sat in the car, he once again closed his eyes and took a deep breath. He was about to start the car and head out into the jungle of a packed freeway. He confidently reached out to turn the key. It took a few seconds for reality to sink into his dulled brain. His ears couldn't believe what they weren't hearing. There wasn't even a groan from his brand-new battery. For some reason, it was dead! It was all too much for Joe. The vase shattered. Yesterday's curse word wasn't strong enough to express how he felt. With his teeth gritted and his eyes bulging, he spat out, "Jesus Christ!"

The question arises as to why Joe should use the name of a *person* in that situation. It does seem to make some sense that he would use an unclean word to express disgust, but why use the name of Jesus Christ? Why didn't he say, "Buddha!" or "Napoleon!"? What's so special about the name of Jesus?

To answer that question, we have to go to the only source of information on the subject—the Bible. In it we see that God has "highly exalted Him [Jesus] and given Him the name which is above every name" (Philippians 2:9). According to the Bible, there is no other name on this earth that deserves more honor and respect than the name of Jesus Christ. When Joe used it in the way he did, he was substituting it for the word beginning with "s." In other words, Joe aligns the holy name with excrement. He counts them as the same—dung. The Bible calls this "blasphemy," and it warns "the LORD will not hold him guiltless who takes His name in vain." In fact, Jesus said, "The world...hates Me because I testify of it that its works are evil" (John 7:7).

I once heard a respected political commentator remark about how a certain party had made phone calls to seniors in Florida. They tried to alarm them about another political party's policy on Social Security. He said that they were trying to "scare the 'B-Jesus' out of them!" What greater verbal expression of hatred can there be for someone than to use the person's name in such a context? Humanity doesn't even use the name of Hitler to curse. His name is not despised with the venomous hatred needed to qualify it for such use.

Most who use God's name in blasphemy would deny that they are using it in the way I have described. In fact, when they blaspheme they will often say they don't even know they are doing it. To them it's "just a word." If that is your justification, then your own mouth condemns you. You so count the name of God as nothing that it passes by your lips without even registering in your mind—you truly use it "in vain." Don't you realize what you are doing? You are cursing the name of the very One who gave you life. Penalty under the Law for blasphemy is death.

The Fourth Commandment tells us, "Remember the Sabbath day, to keep it holy." I ignored this command for twenty-two years of my non-Christian life. Not for a second did I say, "God gave me life; what does He therefore require of me?" let alone set aside one day in seven to worship Him in spirit and in truth. Death is the sentence under the Law for Sabbath breaking.

The Fifth Commandment is, "Honor your father and your mother." That means we are commanded to value them implicitly in a way that is pleasing in the sight of God. Have you *always* honored your parents in a way that's pleasing in God's sight? Have you always had a perfect attitude in all things toward them? Ask God to remind you of some of the sins of your youth. You may have forgotten them, but God hasn't.

> YOU ARE CURSING THE NAME OF THE VERY ONE WHO GAVE YOU LIFE.

What is your most valuable possession? Isn't it your life? Your car, your eyes, your money, and other things are all useless if you are dead. If you are in your right mind, you will want to live a long and happy life. Yet you have God's promise that if you don't honor you parents, you will have neither (Ephesians 6:1–3).

The Sixth Commandment is, "You shall not murder." But Jesus warned that if we get angry without cause, we are in danger of judgment. If we hate our brother, God calls us a murderer. We can violate the spirit of the Law by our attitude and intent.

Perhaps you have the blood of abortion on your hands. Civil law may smile on your crime but God's Law calls you a murderer and the Sixth Commandment demands your death.

The Seventh Commandment is, "You shall not commit adultery." Who of us can say that we are pure, when Jesus said we violate this command in spirit by lusting after another person. He warned, "You have heard that it was said to those of old, 'You shall not commit adultery.' But I say to you that whoever looks at a woman to lust for her has already committed adultery with her in his heart" (Matthew 5:27,28). Until you find peace with God, you will be like a man who steals a TV set. He enjoys the programs, but deep in his heart is the knowledge that at any moment there could be a knock on the door, and the law could bring him to justice.

After I debated at their national convention, the American Atheists published an interview with William B. Davis, who is "best known as the infamous 'smoking man' in the hit television series *The X-Files*." Mr. Davis (a professing atheist) spoke on the subject of the differences between men and women. He said, "Take that guy Comfort, did he really say— he did really say!—that if I looked at a woman with lust in my heart, even if I didn't do anything about it, I'd be damned for eternity, or I've committed adultery. I'm hard-wired for it!" Mr. Davis is right. He is "hard-wired" for sin. It's in his nature. Like every other person, he is a slave to his own base but pleasurable passions.

Remember that God has seen every sin you've ever committed. He has seen the deepest thoughts and desires of your heart. Nothing is hidden from His pure eyes. The day will come when you will have to face that Judge whose Law you have broken. The Scriptures say that the impure (those who are not pure in heart), the immoral (fornicators—those who have sex before marriage), and adulterers will not enter the kingdom of God. Adultery carries the death penalty.

The Eighth Commandment is, "You shall not steal." Have you ever taken something that belonged to someone else? Then you are a thief, and you cannot enter God's kingdom. You may have stolen a book from a library, failed to pay a parking fine, or maybe "borrowed" something and never returned it. God is not impressed with the value of what you stole. When you have stolen, you have sinned against God, and you have violated His Law. Thieves will not inherit the kingdom of God.

The Ninth Commandment is, "You shall not bear false witness." Have you ever told a fib, a "white lie," a half-truth, or an exaggeration? Then you have lied. How many lies do you have to tell to be a liar? Just one, and the Bible warns, "All liars shall have their part in the lake which burns with fire and brimstone" (Revelation 21:8). The Scriptures cannot be broken. We may not think that deceitfulness is a serious sin, but God does.

The final nail in our coffin is *the Tenth Commandment:* "You shall not covet." This means we should not desire things that belong to others. Who of us can say we are innocent? *All* of us have sinned. As the Scriptures say, "There is none righteous, no, not one; there is none who understands; there is none who seeks after God" (Romans 3:10,11). You don't have to break ten of man's laws to be a lawbreaker. The Bible warns, "Whoever shall keep the whole Law, and yet stumble in one point, he is guilty of all" (James 2:10). The most blind of us will usually admit that man has glaring faults. We are forever transgressing against each other. But our true transgressions are vertical, not horizontal. Our real crimes are against God, not man.

If you are brought before a judge and accused of committing a serious crime, he will ask you, "Do you understand the charges that are being brought against you?" I ask you the same question on behalf of the Judge of the universe—do you understand the charges that are being brought against you? Do you see the serious nature of your transgression?

Without the Law, we look at sin from man's standard. We have a distorted view. It takes the Law to give us insight into God's standard, which is utter perfection.

The Bible says, "Who may ascend into the hill of the LORD?...He who has clean hands and a pure heart" (Psalm 24:3,4), and "Blessed are the pure in heart, for they shall see God" (Matthew 5:8). Jesus instructs us to "be perfect, just as your Father in heaven is perfect" (Matthew 5:48).

How do you measure up? Are you perfect, pure, holy, just, and good? Or have you caught a glimpse of what you must look like to God? The picture the Scriptures paint of us is not a nice one.

Diamonds or Water?

Let me put it another way. If I offered you a fistful of diamonds or a bucket of cold water, which would you take? The diamonds, of course. (Who in his right mind wouldn't?) But if you were crawling through a desert with blistered lips and a swollen tongue, dying of thirst, and I offered you a fistful of diamonds or a bucket of cold water, you would despise the diamonds and cry, "Give me water—or I'll die!" That is called "circumstantial priorities." Your priorities change according to your circumstances.

Christianity demands a choice between the sparkling diamonds of sin and the cool, clear water of everlasting life. Most people prefer the diamonds of sin, something quite normal for sin-loving humanity. But on Judgment Day their circumstances will radically change. They will find themselves upon their faces in the desert of God's Judgment, about to perish under the burning heat of a Creator who warns us that He's a "consuming fire." They despised the Living Water when it was offered to them in Christ. Now they must face eternal consequences. Those sparkling diamonds they so dearly clutch will suddenly be the glaring evidence for their condemnation.

Years ago, a television advertisement had a deep-voiced commentator ask the sobering question, "What goes through the mind of a driver at the moment of impact in a head-on collision if he's not wearing a seat belt?" As he spoke, the ad showed a dummy without a safety belt reacting in slow motion to a head-on collision. As the dummy moved forward on impact, the steering wheel went right through its skull. Then the commentator somberly continued, "…the steering wheel. You can learn a lot from a dummy. Buckle up!"

> THE WORST THING YOU CAN DO IS TO SAY THAT YOU WILL CHANGE YOUR LIFESTYLE.

How could the censors allow fear tactics? This advertisement struck trepidation in the hearts of motorists. The reason is clear. *They were speaking the truth.* It is a fearful thing to be in a head-on collision when you're not wearing a seat belt.

What I'm telling you is the gospel truth. The Bible warns, "It is a fearful thing to fall into the hands of the living God" (Hebrews 10:31). It is right that you should fear, because you are in danger of eternal damnation. You are going to collide head-on with God's Law. Let Judgment Day play out before your eyes in slow motion. Look closely at the fearful consequences of not buckling yourself into the salvation of God.

This may sound strange, but the worst thing you can do at this point is to say that you will change your lifestyle—that you will, from this day forward, live a good life. Let's say you were actually able to do that. From now on, not only will you always live a good life, but you will also think pure thoughts. However, who is going to forgive your past sins? Can a judge let a murderer go free because he promises to live a good life from now on? No, the lawbreaker is in debt to justice. He must be punished.

Chapter Sixteen

THE REPELLENT

I N THE PREVIOUS chapter, we "tapped the web" of your heart with the stick of God's Law. The reason for this was to see if we could make the ugly spider of your sinful nature reveal itself from his hiding. I trust that he has come out in the open. For the first time you have seen what you are in the sight of a holy God. The Scriptures say, "We are all like an unclean thing" (Isaiah 64:6). The truth is, you have violated the Law a multitude of times. The Law, like a dam of eternal justice, has been cracked in numerous places and is towering over your head, waiting to burst upon you. The Bible says that the wrath of God abides on you. Jesus warned that if the stone of a just and holy God falls on you, it will "grind you to powder." When you grind something to powder, you do a thorough job. Every foul skeleton in the closet of every human heart will be brought out on the Day of Judgment.

The thought may have entered your mind that perhaps God will *overlook* your sins. Perhaps He, in His mercy, could just look the other way. If He does so, then He is unjust. Again, in civil law a judge cannot look the other way when a criminal is obviously guilty, and be true to what is right. Even if the judge feels sorry for the criminal, he must stay true to the law. Justice must be done. In the ten years between 1980 and 1990, in the United States alone, more than 60,000 murders were committed in which the murderers got away totally free. No doubt the figure is higher as many "accidents" and "suicides" are actually murders in disguise. These are people who have raped, tortured, and strangled helpless victims. Should God overlook their crimes on Judgment Day? Should He turn a blind eye? Should He compromise Eternal Justice?

Perhaps you think God should punish only the serious crimes. But your lying, stealing, adultery of the heart, and rebellion *are* serious in His sight. The Bible says He will by no means clear the guilty. Who would like to see justice overlooked? Isn't it the guilty?

What then is the punishment for sin? It is everlasting damnation. The Scriptures speak of a place called hell. Imagine if God's place of punishment were just a place of continual thirst. Have you ever had thirst where you thought you'd die for lack of liquid? Or imagine if it were only a place of gnawing hunger, or merely chronic toothache? Have you ever been in pain to such an extent that you wanted to die? Have you ever felt the agony of a broken arm, leg, or rib? Have you wakened from a nightmare and been so gripped by terror that it took ten minutes to recover from its hold? Our pains in this life are temporary, but the Bible warns of "everlasting punishment." It will be a place of "weeping and gnashing of teeth," a place where death cannot bring welcome relief to suffering. God will withdraw every blessing He has showered upon sinful, rebellious, ungrateful humanity. Can you begin to imagine a place where there will be absence of light, color, goodness, peace, beauty, love, and laughter? It is an abode of darkness, depression, and despair. A terror-filled place, where those who have murdered, raped, tortured, stolen, lied, hated, been greedy, lustful, envious, jeal-

> PERHAPS YOU THINK GOD SHOULD PUNISH ONLY THE SERIOUS CRIMES.

ous, blasphemous, and rebellious will dwell. Hell is the place where sinful humanity will receive its just retribution for crimes against the Law of a holy God. How terrible sin must be in the sight of God to merit such just punishment.

I intensely dislike saying such things. I would rather say, "Please don't go to hell," but they are empty words to sin-loving humanity. Many times I have had people say, "I don't mind going to hell." To them, the sparkling diamonds of sin are far more attractive that the cool, clear waters of God's mercy. My only course is to "hang you out of the plane by your ankles," in the hope that fear for your soul will do its necessary work.

How's your conscience? Is it doing its duty? Is it accusing you of sin? Is it affirming the Commandments as being right? If not, which of the Commandments do you feel are unjust? "You shall not steal," "You shall not bear false witness," "You shall not murder"? Perhaps you have committed adultery, or you have been longing for an opportunity to do so. While no human being can point an accusing finger at you, the ten fingers of God's Holy Law stand as your accuser. You have been caught holding a smoking gun. The Law calls for your blood. Under it, the penalty for adultery is death by stoning. I don't stand as your accuser; I hang my head in guilt as one who has been in your place. Like every other red-blooded male, I too was an adulterer at heart. I cannot, in good conscience, call for justice to take its course.

Caught in the Act

You are like the woman caught in the very act of adultery. The ten great rocks of the Law are waiting to crush the life from you. My earnest prayer is that you won't attempt to justify yourself, but bow your head and agree with the Law and the impartial voice of your conscience, and say, "Guilty!

What must I do to be saved?" In doing so, you are merely saying that God's testimony about humanity is true, that our hearts are deceitfully wicked to a point of not only being vile sinners, but of being so deceitful that we are loath to admit our own sins.

Like the woman, you have no other avenue to take. Your only hope is to fall at the feet of the Son of God. Ironically, there is only One human being who can call for justice to be done. Yet He is the only One who can forgive sins. Only at His feet is the Law satisfied. If you humbly call on His name, you will hear, "Has no one condemned you?" and be able to say, like the woman, "No one, Lord."

Hopefully, the Law has stirred up the judge of your conscience. In the past you could sin and not be concerned, because the judge had been wooed into a deep slumber. The thunderings of the Law awoke him and now he also stands as your accuser. There is an air of indignation that he has been silenced for so long. He awakened from his sleep with a vengeance, and with each Commandment he says, "Guilty!" What then must you do to satisfy his charges? No monetary payment will quiet his accusation of liability. No prison sentence will silence his righteous charge. What is it that will free you from the torments of what the world calls a "guilty conscience"?

The Bible says that there is only one thing that can do it. It is the blood of Jesus Christ: "How much more shall the blood of Christ, who through the eternal Spirit offered Himself without spot to God, *cleanse your conscience from dead works* to serve the living God?" (Hebrews 9:14, emphasis added). In other words, anything you might try to do to save yourself from the consequences of sin is nothing but "dead works."

Let's go back to civil law. Imagine that you have broken

the law and are guilty of some terrible crime. You don't have two beans to rub together. There's nothing you can do to redeem yourself. Justice is about to take its course, when someone you don't even know steps into the courtroom and pays the fine for you. If that happens, the demands of the law are totally satisfied by the one who paid your fine. You are free to go from the courtroom. That's what God did for you. When the Law condemned us, Jesus Christ stepped into the courtroom and paid the fine for us by His own precious blood.

When the Law called for our blood, Jesus gave His. When Eternal Justice cried out for retribution, Jesus cried out on the cross in agony as He satisfied it. The Law didn't just demand the death of the Son of God; it demanded the *suffering* death of the sinless Savior. Sin is so serious in the sight of God that the only way to satisfy His righteousness was by the unspeakable suffering of a sinless sacrifice.

I once heard the story of an African chief who got wind of a planned mutiny. In an effort to quash the revolt, he called the tribe together. He then warned them that anyone caught in rebellion would be given 100 lashes, without mercy.

A short time later, to the chief's dismay, he found that his own brother was at the bottom of the revolt. He wanted to be head of the tribe. Everyone thought the chief would break his word. But being a just man, he had his brother tied to a tree. He then had himself tied next to him, and he took those 100 lashes across his own bare flesh. In doing so, he not only kept his word—justice was done—but he also demonstrated his great love toward his brother.

When God became flesh in the Messiah and suffered on the cross, He was not only satisfying His justice, but He was also demonstrating the depth of His love toward us. Can you imagine how that brother felt as the chief took the punishment that was due to him? Can you understand that every lash of the whip would break his rebellious heart? Can you see tears well in his eyes, and his face wince as he heard each lash of the whip? Is your own heart so hard that you can hear the nails being driven into the hands of the Son of God, and not be moved by such love? Isn't there a cry in your own heart, as you hear the agonies of the cross? Or have you a heart of stone? He suffered in our place, taking our punishment. May God make it real to you.

Let's go back to the plane analogy for a moment. Imagine if I had spent a great deal of effort in trying to persuade you to put your parachute on. I spoke to you about the horrific consequences of breaking the law of gravity. I had been hanging you out of the plane by your ankles, speaking of what would happen to you if you hit the ground at 120 miles per hour. Your eyes widened as I covered the details. It slowly dawned on you that if you wanted to live, you had better put the parachute on. Suddenly, you are convinced. You need no more words from me. With trembling hands, you reach under your seat *and find that there is no parachute.* Fear begins to grip you as you think of the terrible death you must face at any moment. As you sit in a daze, you are awakened from your nightmare by a kindly voice. Another stranger is offering you a parachute. You reach out and take it in your trembling hands. Words can't express your gratitude. An unspeakable joy fills your heart as you realize that you don't have to die. Any thought about where the stranger obtained the parachute doesn't enter your mind.

YOU HAVE NO OTHER OPTION. UNLESS YOU REPENT, YOU SHALL PERISH.

After the jump, you find that all the other passengers landed safely. All but one. It is only then that you realize the stranger gave you his own parachute. He went to his death so that you could live.

That is what Jesus Christ did for you. He gave His life so that you could live. A complete Stranger, someone you didn't even know, did that for you. His was a willing, terrible, substitutionary death.

What Then Should You Do?

What you must do is obey the command of God to repent. Then you must put your trust in Jesus Christ. You must be born again (John 3:7). Your alternative is to have the full fury of God's Law unleashed against you on Judgment Day. You have no other option. Unless you repent, you shall perish. There is only One person who has defeated death. It was not possible for the grave to hold Jesus of Nazareth. There is no purgatory, no second chance, no other name, no other hope, no other way for you to be saved. God offers you forgiveness of sins and the gift of everlasting life. Pray a prayer like this from your heart:

> "Dear God, I have violated Your Law. I have broken Your Commandments. I have sinned against You. You have seen my every thought and deed. You saw the sins of my youth, and the unclean desires of my heart. I am truly sorry. I now understand how serious my transgressions have been. If justice was to be done, and all my sins uncovered on the Day of Judgment, I know I would be guilty, and justly end up in hell. Words cannot express my gratitude for the cross of the Lord Jesus Christ. I may not have a tear in my eye, but there is one in my heart. I really am sorry for my sins. From this

day forward, I will show my gratitude for Your mercy by living a life that is pleasing in Your sight. I will read Your Word daily and obey what I read. In Jesus' name I pray, amen."

Chapter Seventeen

A HOPEFUL PRESUMPTION

I AM GOING TO make a hopeful presumption. I am hoping that you have made a commitment of your life to Jesus Christ. Now I want to share with you some very important thoughts in the following chapters. If you are already a Christian, please read on because what I am going to say also concerns you.

If you have made a commitment, God will prove Himself faithful to you, as He has to millions of others through the ages. All that is required is your obedience. Read the Bible daily. Believe His promises, remembering that there is no greater insult to God than not to take Him at His Word.

Hang in There

There was once a daring escape from a Nazi war prison. The inmates had dug a tunnel but had miscalculated. The tunnel surfaced twenty feet short of the cover of a wooded area. They waited until a moonless night, then sent one man through the tunnel and into the woods to watch for the time when the guard turned his back. The escapee's job was to pull on a piece of string that ran from the woods into the tunnel. This would let the next prisoner know it was safe for him to emerge.

One by one, the men felt the tug of the string and surfaced, running into the safety of the dark woods. At one point, the guard heard a sound and walked across to the area of the hole. He didn't see the opening, but stood by it for some time, looking around suspiciously. Time seemed to stand still for the next prisoner who was waiting underground for the tug on the string.

Suddenly, he lost patience. He could stand it no longer. He moved forward, then up and out of the hole in the dark. It was the last thing he did. The guard swung around and fired on him with his machine gun.

We can learn from that man's fatal mistake. His error was threefold. He lacked patience, faith, and obedience. If only he had trusted the person on the other end, if only he had obeyed the instructions given to him, he would have found his freedom. Instead, he lost his very life.

PRIDE IS A SIN THAT WILL STOP MULTITUDES FROM ENTERING THE KINGDOM OF HEAVEN.

The Bible tells us that we inherit the promises of God through "faith and patience." There will be times in your Christian walk when you will ask God for something, and there will be a delay. Don't lose patience. Wait on the Lord. The One holding onto the string can see things you can't. He knows what is best for you. Obey His Instruction Book and "trust in the LORD with all your heart, and lean not on your own understanding" (Proverbs 3:5). Don't trust your judgments or your emotions.

If you have repented and trusted in Christ, you are now in a different kingdom—God's kingdom. God does things totally different from the way you have been accustomed. Becoming a Christian is like leaving your native country and moving to another. There are radical culture shocks.

In 1989, our family moved 8,000 miles from New Zealand to the United States. Although our country is similar to the U.S., we did find that there was a slight culture shock. Down Under, we drive on the other side of the road. The change from "left means life, right means death" to the opposite is fairly simple—until you come to an intersection and have to make a left turn. Only once (in the first week) did I drive on the wrong side of the road. Sue gently screamed, which told me something was wrong.

There are a few other minor differences. In New Zealand, cars have the steering wheel on the opposite side. After coming out of a supermarket, I opened the door, sat in my vehicle, and wondered who on earth would want to steal my steering wheel. When I quickly realized my mistake, I felt more foolish than anything. My pride had been hurt. I pretended that I was playing around in the glove compartment until I was sure that no one had seen my little error.

Pane in the Nose

Pride is a subtle thing. I remember many years ago stepping forward to take a closer look at a sofa in a shop display. Suddenly I came to an abrupt halt. I had walked straight into a plate glass door. Did I give thought to the pain coming from my flattened nose? No. My first thought was, *Who saw me?* When I realized that no one had seen the incident, I proceeded to give comfort to my nose.

I once saw a woman walk behind me while I was preaching outdoors. As she did so, she stumbled and twisted her ankle. It apparently didn't hurt at all. With the utmost composure, she graciously walked across in front of the crowd as though nothing had happened. Yet from my viewpoint I could see that when she got around the corner, she doubled up with pain.

The Bible says God hates pride. It is a sin that will stop multitudes from entering the kingdom of heaven. Pride destroys families. It stops spouses from admitting that they are wrong. They would rather break up a family and keep their pride, than humble themselves and be reconciled, even for the sake of the children.

There were more blows to my pride. Other adjustments in our move to the U.S. were relatively minor. Down Under, light switches are up for "off," and down for "on." The sun goes across on the other side of the sky. When it's summer here, it's winter there. The accent is different. The water goes down the drain the opposite way. A check on a form means "right" and a "cross" means "wrong." Also, Down Under, a "fag" is a cigarette butt, not a homosexual. This last colloquialism is minor until one uses the word while preaching. I was preaching open air in Hawaii when a drunken heckler began yelling at me. He called himself a Christian, even though he was drunk and had a cigarette hanging from his mouth. After a bit of an exchange, much to my consternation he began to leave, so I called, "Going off for another fag, huh?" The crowd roared, and I was left bewildered. Afterwards, I was filled in about why I had received that response.

Another similar incident happened when I was asked to give blood at the local Red Cross. When we arrived, I spent quite some time filling out a form about my background. The AIDS virus had left blood banks in justifiable paranoia. Ordinary banks are worried about bad withdrawals; blood banks are worried about bad deposits. The list seemed endless: had I ever had AIDS, did I have heart disease, did I have fainting spells, etc. I looked down the long list, then across to the boxes on the right side of the form. It was simple. All they contained were "Yes" and "No," so I went down the boxes and did what all good people from Down Under do: I crossed out the non-applicable ones. Did I have AIDS? I crossed out the "Yes" in the box, leaving a clear "No" for the person marking the form. It made sense to me.

I then took the form to the nurse and sat beside her. She stared at it for about three seconds before looking at me in horror. My marks on the form indicated that I had AIDS, hepatitis, typhoid, malaria, cancer, heart disease, lumps under my arms, skin rashes, fainting spells, and that I'd had diarrhea for over a month—among a number of other distasteful things.

Her facial expression changed when I told her that New Zealanders walk around upside-down, drive on the other side of the road, and fill out forms differently.

> YOU ARE NOW LIVING IN A KINGDOM WHOSE RULES ARE REVOLUTIONARY.

So, in one sense, you have (by way of your commitment to Christ) moved into a radically different culture. You are now living in a kingdom whose rules are revolutionary. You have bowed your knee to the sovereignty of the King of kings. Now you owe your allegiance to Him—above all else—and His ways are certainly different. No man ever spoke like Jesus. He said to love your enemies, turn the other cheek, and do good to those who hate you. Many have missed the point of why the Christian should let another person stomp on him. The reason is not that the Christian is a wimp, but that he has surrendered the job of vengeance to the Lord. If someone does me wrong, I am not to take matters into my own hands. Instead, I give it all to God in prayer, and if (in His perfect judgment) He sees fit to do so, He will stomp on the person who stomped on me; and He has a righteous (and bigger) stomp.

Let me give you some examples of how this works. Sue and I used to sell our books and tapes on a credit system.

After a seminar, if people didn't have any money at the time, we would let them take what they wanted, and we would send them a bill. It was a good system, except that after awhile we discovered there were $3,000 worth of unpaid bills. Professing Christians were taking our property and not paying for it. We sent reminders. That didn't produce any response at all. So we decided we would get radical and do it God's way. We mailed a gift of ten dollars to each of those who had stolen books and tapes from us, based on the fact that Jesus said to do good to those who spitefully use you. He said that if someone wants to take your tunic, you should give the person your cloak also (Matthew 5:40). What we were saying was, "God, we give it all to You. We want You to be our financial adviser. If You see fit to stomp on these people, that's up to You. You know their circumstances. Perhaps they are in financial difficulty. In the meantime, we will love our neighbors as ourselves and do them good."

The following weekend, I did a series of meetings for a church, and found that the honorarium they gave me was ten times the normal amount! We like the way God works, so now we do things His way.

This wasn't just an isolated incident. I once sent fourteen boxes of books to South Africa. When they arrived, the person who ordered them called to say they were all damaged. We were 4,000 miles apart, so all I could do was to ask him to claim the insurance. For some reason, he refused. A friend told me to instigate court proceedings, but I felt led to draw on the wisdom of my Business Adviser. So I gave the whole thing to God in prayer and dismissed it. The next weekend at a Christian camp, we sold more than seven times as many books and tapes as we usually sell.

A close friend of mine was a partner in a Christian T-shirt company. One of their shirts had a particular word on it that was used by a well-known apparel company. Not long after the shirt was released, the apparel company threatened to sue my friend's company for using the word unless they came up with a quick $10,000. Even though their lawyers felt there was no way they could lose the case in court, he prayed about it and felt led to obey the Scriptures. Because Jesus said that if someone sues you for your coat you should give him your cloak also, he gave them a number of checks (over a short period) totaling $10,000, then an extra $1,000 check.

What he did didn't make sense. Yet within one month, God had so blessed the T-shirt company that they expanded from eight employees to forty-two. In fact, within three years of business, they sold over 1,000,000 T-shirts.

You may not be involved in book or T-shirt sales, but you can put these same principles into practice. If someone does you wrong, stop for a minute and ask, "What would man have me do, and what would Jesus have me do?" Man's way is to stick up for your rights. That will be a way that feels good to your natural mind, a way that *seems* right—but give it all to God in prayer, then do it His way.

If someone wrongs you at work, buy him a gift. Do the person good, and then pray that through God's love his heart will be open to the claims of the gospel.

Chapter Eighteen

WATCH AND PRAY

ONCE WHEN I was preaching open air someone called out, "If you were a Christian, you would give me your watch." So, without being distracted from what I was saying, I slipped off my watch and handed it to him. I forgot that the watch had "American Revival—pray without ceasing" printed across its face. When he saw it, I was told later that he made the "sign of a cross" and gave it to someone else to give back to me. I wonder what upset him? Was it the word "Revival"?

Most non-Christians don't know what the word "revival" means. It has even lost its sense in many contemporary Christian circles. To many, it means no more than a sweating, tie-loosened preacher, stirring up a congregation for two or three nights. There is much singing, many decisions, then everyone goes home and all is forgotten in a few weeks. True revival is a sovereign move of God, such as what happened in Wales at the turn of the century. So many were converted that the police were out of work. Bars were empty. Even the coal miners' mules had to be retrained because their owners were no longer cursing and speaking harshly to them. Now they were gentle and loving, and the mules didn't recognize the commands.

Once while showering, I was meditating on all the problems besetting the United States. I thought about the millions of abortions, the murders, violence, family breakdowns, spousal abuse, child molestations, rape, greed, rampant diseases, sky-rocketing suicide rates, floods, earthquakes, loneliness, fear, suffering, pain, and the fear of death that is tormenting humanity. Then I thought about the terror of Judgment Day and the inevitability of hell for those who reject God's mercy. My mind seemed to reel in confusion about what I should do as a Christian. Suddenly, I looked up at the shower unit. It was one of those pulsating heads with the instructions printed around the outside. These instructions were different, though. Somehow they had been caught when the unit turned, leaving nothing but a jumbled mess. There were e's and a's, y's and p's. Nothing made sense. It was just a mass of disarray, except for one word. The "s" had been scraped off the word "spray," leaving alone among the confusion the word "pray."

As Christians, that is what you and I can do to help the United States. We all can pray. A great preacher once said, "What constitutes a spirit of prayer? Is it many prayers and warm words? No, it is a state of continual desire and anxiety of mind for the salvation of sinners." That should be the basic attitude of mind within every Christian. But what is it that we should be requesting of God? There are the daily necessities of life, our "daily bread," etc., but Jesus also told us specifically to pray for "laborers." That's what is needed to bring revival to America. A laborer is one who is prepared to go out into the harvest fields and sweat for the kingdom of God. While there are thousands in the U.S. who are laboring for God, many have been left without the needed "sickle"— because of ignorance they are trying to reap with their bare hands.

You may be familiar with the "soap bubble" message of the modern gospel. It is one that promises love, joy, peace, and fulfillment to those who give their lives to Jesus Christ.

In truth, the promise of Scripture for those who follow Jesus is tribulation, temptation, persecution,...and everlasting life. The last one is the frosting on the cake, making the first three bearable.

One thing I feel I am called to do (with the help of God) is to burst the soap bubble, then encourage the Church back to the biblical presentation of the way of salvation. Instead of telling sinners that Jesus will make them happy, we must warn them that God's wrath is abiding on them and that they need to repent. The correct way to do this is to use the Law of God to bring the knowledge of sin. That is what I have endeavored to do in this book, so review the different chapters and familiarize yourself with the way this is done.[12] You need to do this so that you can be effective as a laborer. It is vital for you to have a concern for the lost, not only for their sake, but also for yours. Love for your neighbor's eternal welfare is one sign that you have been converted. When you are born again, you receive a new heart with new desires. You will naturally love God, and you will also naturally love your neighbor. This is because God promised that He would put His Law into our hearts, causing us to do the things that please Him. While in an unconverted state, it was "natural" for us to walk in rebellion to His will. Now, because of the new birth, it is *naturally* our delight to want to fulfill His desires. This means that, as you see the plight of the lost, you will want to share with them the way of salvation.

> WHEN YOU ARE BORN AGAIN, YOU RECEIVE A NEW HEART WITH NEW DESIRES.

Laborers are desperately needed. America is in trouble; even the secular world knows that. Drug lords, like devouring beasts, are tearing at her fleshly borders. She is bleeding from without, and broken and bruised from within. Her youth, the very future of the nation, are being destroyed by sin and shame. Thirty-three thousand youth get some sort of sexually transmitted disease *each day*, with 1.2 million becoming pregnant each year. Despite easy access to free sex and other temporal pleasures, thousands each year are mystifying experts by choosing the escape of suicide. The suicide rate in the United States has tripled in the last three decades. About 100,000 Americans less than 25 years of age attempt suicide each year; 5,000 succeed. Suicide is the third leading cause of death in youths 15 to 24 years of age and the fifth leading cause of death in adults aged 25 to 64 years. In total, nearly 30,000 Americans commit suicide annually.

Corruption among morally blind political leaders can only take the U.S. into the "ditch." Jesus warned that both leaders and followers would fall. The unthinkable is happening —families are more than disintegrating. Parents are murdering their children; husbands are killing their wives. Despite a recent poll in *TV Guide* revealing that ninety-six percent of Americans believe in God, rape, racial violence, murder, theft, gambling, adultery, and abortion are rampant. Pornographic video producers can hardly feed the demand. Twenty million pornographic magazines are sold *each week*. The most popular movies carry warnings that they need parental guidance; in other words, they contain perversions, sex, foul language, blasphemy, and violence. In fact, the average sixteen-year-old American has seen 200,000 acts of violence and 32,000 murders through the mediums of television and movies.

Homosexuality is now viewed as an acceptable alternative lifestyle, with 100,000 gays living in San Francisco and an estimated 4 million nationwide. The plague of AIDS has not only taken tens of thousands of homosexuals to a humiliating and agonizing death, it has inundated the heterosexual community. In the late seventies, godless judges opened the floodgates of the murderous practice of abortion, which has taken the lives of over 40 million unborn Americans. Despite the nation's supposed belief in God, it is estimated that 140 million shoplifting offenses occur each year. Way back in 1987, 13 million video recorders were stolen, every seventy-eight seconds a person was robbed, every five minutes someone was raped, every thirty-three seconds a car was stolen, and every ten seconds a burglar struck. Over 40 million Americans are the victims of violent crime each year. So many law-breakers are packed into U.S. prisons that judges are being forced to release guilty criminals back onto the street after they've served only a fraction of their sentence.

Throughout the nation, sad and pathetic photos of kidnapped beloved children are displayed in the hope that they will be returned before they are sexually abused or used in some horrific satanic ritual. Schoolchildren are gunned down while at school or molested in the classroom or at home. Anti-Semitic Nazism and racial hatred boil beneath the surface of the nation, waiting to explode. Thousands of homeless persons roam the streets, enslaved to alcohol or drugs. Millions of people are trapped by fear—fear of their fellow man, fear of the future, fear of cancer, fear of the all-too-common earthquakes, droughts, tornadoes, and floods.

Wide Open Doors

Meanwhile, despite America's 1,485 Christian radio stations and over 300 Christian television stations, the "salt of the earth" is being trampled underfoot. Back in 1988, a leading Christian magazine conducted a confidential survey among 300 pastors. In the survey, twenty-three percent admitted that they had been involved in some sort of sexual immorality.

That's one in five *pastors!* If that's the state of the shepherds, what must the flocks be like?

The problem is that the Church has forsaken the true message of salvation, that the way into the kingdom of God is a "straight gate" and a "narrow way." We have made the issue one of happiness, rather than righteousness. Then, with manipulative music and appeals to the emotions rather than the will and conscience, we have opened wide our doors to the world and its sins. We have sown our own seed, telling people that the way of entry is broad and easy. As a consequence we have reaped a "mixed multitude," as evidenced by the condition of the contemporary Church.

The typical state of many professing Christians was seen recently on a program that was broadcast worldwide. When a well-known Christian, who previously hosted a TV talk show, spoke of tough times she had been through, she related that actor Kevin Costner had called to tell her that she was a shining light in a dark world. Then he told her, "Greater is he that is in you than he that is in the world." The woman said she was surprised that he would know a Bible verse, and found out that he had learned it in Sunday school. I was delighted that she had boldly quoted God's Word on a program that was watched by millions. Then the host said, "We've got five seconds. I hear you are doing a movie. Tell us about it." She concluded by saying, "I act the part of a nymphomaniac, who's a real b-i-t-c-h."

A Free Facial

Today, from within the army of God come many uncertain sounds. There are trumpet calls from "peace and safety" to gloom and judgment, and the irony is that both extremes are coming from spiritually respected sources. Some are saying that America's sexual sins are worse than those of Sodom and

Gomorrah, or that she is beyond redemption. Others carry on with a positive confession of prosperity as though all were well.

A number of years ago, I ran a series of advertisements on television in which I attempted to warn parents about occult music that advocated murder. After screening the ads, I wondered if I would end up getting my face rearranged. I was sitting in my parked car a week later when a gentleman, with his fist clenched and a determined look on his face, walked up to my car and asked, "Are you Ray Comfort?" After I acknowledged that I was, he thrust his hand through the open window, dropped twenty dollars in my lap, and walked off—much to my relief. I guess it was his way of saying, "Thanks."

THE CHURCH HAS FORSAKEN THE TRUE MESSAGE OF SALVATION.

It would seem that God delights in bringing victory out of disastrous situations. As Israel stood helplessly by the Red Sea, trapped by their enemies with no possible way of escape, God did the impossible. With Daniel, God brought victory out of disaster. With Lazarus, He did the impossible by raising him from the dead. What great horror, darkness, hopelessness, and death surrounded the hill of Calvary, yet from it came the ultimate, glorious victory of the resurrection. To say that America is in a dark, hopeless state is the understatement of the century. Satan holds America in his cold, clenched iron fist in resolute rebellion. His work is blatantly evident—disease, crime, fear, violence, greed, murder, rape, pornography, suicide, adultery, corruption, alcoholism, drug addiction, racism, the occult, marriage breakdown—just to name a few. Add to this God's anger against sin, and the situation looks disastrous. Yet God in His sovereignty can, in a moment of time, open Satan's iron grip and drop the riches of revival into the lap of the Church.

Meanwhile, we must each obey the divine Commandment to "lift up your voice like a trumpet; tell [this] people their transgression" (Isaiah 58:1). Let us work with God's Holy Spirit, and allow Him to pray through us in travailing prayer with "groanings that cannot be uttered," that God might bring to birth His purposes in the closing hours of time. Let's forget our past failings, and through faith look beyond the Red Sea, past the lions' mouths, etc., for with God nothing shall be impossible (Matthew 19:26).

Chapter Nineteen

THE LOST ALTAR

THE FOLLOWING information will be of interest to you if you have had parents: A new scientific study has revealed that, if your parents didn't have children, neither will you.

As we have just seen in the previous chapter, America is in the midst of dark days. Why is the U.S. in such a dilemma? The reason is very clear:

> Give ear, O my people, to my law; incline your ears to the words of my mouth. I will open my mouth in a parable; I will utter dark sayings of old, which we have heard and known, and our fathers have told us.
>
> We will not hide them from their children, telling to the generation to come the praises of the LORD, and His strength and His wonderful works that He has done. For He established a testimony in Jacob, and appointed a law in Israel, which He commanded our fathers, that they should make them known to their children; that the generation to come might know them, the children who would be born, that they may arise and declare them to their children, that they may set their hope in God, and not forget the works of God, but keep His commandments; and may not be like their fathers, a stubborn and rebellious generation, a generation that did not set its heart aright, and whose spirit was not faithful to God (Psalm 78:1–8).

Notice how Israel was told to make the Law of God known

to their children. Now look at Deuteronomy 6:6 (just after the Law was given to Moses) and see the same admonition:

> And these words which I command you today shall be in your heart. You shall teach them diligently to your children, and shall talk of them when you sit in your house, when you walk by the way, when you lie down, and when you rise up. You shall bind them as a sign on your hand, and they shall be as frontlets between your eyes. You shall write them on the doorposts of your house and on your gates.

In Old Testament times, people sometimes built an altar to God to commemorate something God had done. Altars also served as a memorial to tell others about God and His character. Joshua writes about one occasion when an altar was built to teach succeeding generations:

> Those twelve stones which they took out of the Jordan, Joshua set up in Gilgal. Then he spoke to the children of Israel, saying: "When your children ask their fathers in time to come, saying, 'What are these stones?' then you shall let your children know, saying, 'Israel crossed over this Jordan on dry land'; for the LORD your God dried up the waters of the Jordan before you until you had crossed over, as the LORD your God did to the Red Sea, which He dried up before us until we had crossed over, that all the peoples of the earth may know the hand of the LORD, that it is mighty, that you may fear the LORD your God forever" (Joshua 4:20–24).

It is a sad fact that the Church today has lost the family "altar," particularly the teaching of God's Law to our children—and that is perhaps the number-one reason why the Church, and thus America, is in such disarray. It has taken only a generation or two for the moral rot to set in. It wasn't too long ago that the United States could be called a "godly nation," esteeming the Ten Commandments.

Gathering for a family "altar" or a devotional time is a good way to teach our children about God and His ways. With that thought in mind, let's take a firm grip upon eight solid rocks and build a family altar. If you don't have any children, take these solid rocks and pile them into the corners of your mind so that when you have influence over children, they will grow up to bring delight to you and to God.

Pray

First, let's take the solid rock of prayer. It goes without saying that we should begin devotions by prayerfully asking God, "Open my eyes, that I may see wondrous things from Your Law" (Psalm 119:18). The Bible uses the phrase "the Law" to refer at different times to the entire Word of God, the Law of Moses, and the Ten Commandments. The Ten Commandments are the very backbone of Holy Scripture. We must seek the help of God's Holy Spirit if we are to comprehend the incredible things God has in His Law. The apostle Paul said, "I delight in the Law of God" (Romans 7:22). Why should we delight in God's Law,

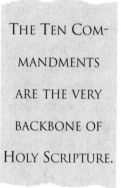

THE TEN COM- MANDMENTS ARE THE VERY BACKBONE OF HOLY SCRIPTURE.

even though we are not saved by our obedience to it? It is because the Law reveals God's holiness, His righteousness, His justice and truth. It is the very instrument that the Holy Spirit uses to convert the soul (Psalm 19:7). It is the means by which the way to the sinner's heart is prepared to receive the grace of God. If we want to see our children truly converted, we must first know the wondrous things from His

Law, and that only comes by prayer and revelation of the Holy Spirit.

Open the Scriptures

The Bible says, "A servant of the Lord must...be able to teach" (2 Timothy 2:24). Don't say, "I can't teach"; say, "Success comes in cans." Memorize this promise from Scripture: "I can do all things through Christ who strengthens me" (Philippians 4:13). If you have young children, start with a "picture" Bible. I did this many years ago when I found a Bible full of beautiful pictures of Adam and Eve, Noah's ark, David and Goliath, etc. But when I turned to the New Testament, I found a picture of King Herod being presented with John the Baptist's head on a plate! John's eyes were vacantly staring into space, and his mouth was gaping open! It was horrible. So, I took some crayons, and (God forgive me) I changed John the Baptist's head into a birthday cake. For years my kids must have been mystified about why King Herod's guests were so horrified at the sight of a cake.

An excellent book if you have kids aged three to twelve years is *Little Visits with God* by Mary Manz Simon (Concordia Publishing). Also, you may like to use *The Evidence—For Kids* (Bridge-Logos).

Place the Law in the Heart

Obey the command of Deuteronomy 6:6 to put the Law of God in your heart, and in the hearts of your children. Have your children memorize the Ten Commandments, and relevant New Testament verses. Your children will never appreciate the cross until they understand the demands of the Law. Why on earth did Jesus die? It was primarily to fulfill the demands of the Law.

Recently, two boys who were fishing tried to cross a swift

stream. As they did so, a log knocked them both into deeper water. One made it to the riverbank but the other got into difficulty. A man saw him and dived in, and after a long while fighting the current, he finally got the boy to the edge of the riverbank. Lifting the lad with both arms, he tossed him onto the bank. A woman grabbed the boy, and watched as the exhausted man sank down into the water. He came up once more, and then drowned. Tragically, he gave his all in saving the boy, and had nothing left to save himself.

Imagine relating the ending of that story to someone without giving the details preceding it: "A man drowned in a river today." The truth is that the danger the boy was in, due to the swiftness of the current, led the man to give his all, showing what concern he had for the boy.

Don't merely tell your kids, "Jesus died for you on the cross." Teach them the reality of salvation. The swift current of Eternal Justice was sweeping all of humanity into the very jaws of hell, but Jesus gave His all to redeem us from the curse of the Law, being made a curse for us. Teach the Law to your children and you will help them appreciate the work of the cross.

Involve the Senses

The more senses involved in the learning environment, the better the lesson will sink in. In a family altar setting, have each person audibly read a verse of the Scriptures. This will have two effects:

- It will build their confidence in reading out loud.

- It will help them remain attentive.

When you hear something, you retain about ten percent of the knowledge imparted. When you see something, you retain about forty-four percent. When you see and hear something, you retain eighty percent. So, after our devotional reading (when the kids were small), we would enjoy role-playing Bible passages. We would act out the raising of Lazarus, Daniel in the lion's den, or David and Goliath. The children were learning biblical principles and having fun at the same time.

Liberally Use Anecdotes

It is said of the Messiah, "I will open my mouth in a parable" (Psalm 78:2). Jesus told stories that carried a deeper meaning. We must do the same. When I was on the East Coast recently, a friend pointed out a restaurant in which a doctor had eaten tuna and developed food poisoning. After the paramedics arrived the doctor said, "Show me the EKG." He took one look at it and said, "I'll be dead in fifteen minutes!" He was right. He had fifteen minutes to find peace with God. I hope he knew the way of salvation.

I heard about a woman who was in a serious car accident. As she lay dying in the hospital, she called for her mother, took her by the hand and said, "Mom you taught me how to sew, how to cook, and how to keep house. You taught me everything about living, but you didn't teach me how to die!" How do you do that? How do you teach a child about death?

Sue and I went to the famed Knotts Berry Farm with my brother-in-law who loves roller-coasters. When he asked me to go on the insane "Montezuma's Revenge," I declined. This ride does a complete 360-degree loop, goes up vertically, and then does the loop backwards!

As he walked through the gates alone, a feeling of sorrow for him clouded my good sense. I also felt embarrassed that my daughter, Rachel, had been on it five times. I gave up my battle and went on it. When the ride ended, my knees were weak. I was consoled by the fact that the first time Rachel went on it she had been terrified too. The second time she was fearful, the third she was worried, the fourth ride she enjoyed, and by the fifth time she was bored. The more she experienced the ride, the less fearful she became. Instead of being paralyzed by fear, she enjoyed herself when she realized that there was nothing to fear. The roller-coaster had proven itself to be trustworthy.

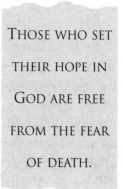

THOSE WHO SET THEIR HOPE IN GOD ARE FREE FROM THE FEAR OF DEATH.

That is the key to teaching your children about death. Why should we teach our children the Law and the "praises of the LORD, and His strength and His wonderful works that He has done"? Because they can learn from the experiences of men and women of God and "set their hope in God." Those who set their hope in God are free from the power and the fear of death.

You may not realize it, but I have just used three anecdotes:

- The man who had fifteen minutes to live

- The mother who taught her daughter about everything but dying

- The roller-coaster experience

Didn't they hold your interest? Follow in the steps of the greatest Teacher, and open your mouth in a parable.

Use Repetition

Repetition is the mother of knowledge. To help our children retain God's Word, we repeated a verse six times with them, then gave them a reward (a candy bar) when they had memorized ten verses. I have calculated that we had around six thousand family devotions with our children. The three of them made it through their teenage years without an ounce of rebellion. This was despite the warnings we were given about the trouble we would have during their teenage years. These principles work.

Share Personal Stories

If you had been sitting in on our family devotions, you probably would have thought that we were getting off the subject. We would speak about how Sue and I met, the kids as babies, school, and a million other things besides the Scriptures. We did this deliberately, so that we would get to know our children, and they would learn more about their parents, each other, and their family history. If we hadn't done this, our children would have been in danger of becoming passing strangers within the home.

Plow Through the Ice Age

Without being legalistic, don't let anything prevent you from having family devotions. Your children will grow out of wanting to play David and Goliath. Around the age of thirteen they will more than likely enter the "ice age." Instead of laughing at your jokes, or giggling as you roll around on the floor, they will sit like blocks of ice. Around that time you will ask yourself, "Is it worth it?" Carry on regardless. You are imparting God's Word, and He will watch over it.

Several years ago, a man wrote a letter to the editor of *The British Weekly*, complaining about not remembering sermons preached in church and questioning whether it was worthwhile. He said, "I have been attending a church service ... for the past thirty years and have heard probably 3,000 sermons. To my consternation I discovered that I cannot remember a single sermon!"

For several weeks many responded to him in the Letters to the Editor column, but the following letter finally settled the issue: "I have been married for thirty years. During that time I have eaten 32,850 meals—mostly of my wife's cooking. Suddenly, I have discovered that I cannot remember the menu of a single meal. And yet, I received nourishment from every single one of them. I have the distinct impression that without them, I would have starved to death long ago."

The Goal of Teaching

We should have a goal as we teach our children. The Bible says, "Now the purpose of the Commandment [the context seems to be speaking of the Law of God] is love from a pure heart, from a good conscience, and from sincere faith" (1 Timothy 1:5). What we were seeking to do (with the help of God) was to produce love and faith, both of which would produce the other fruits of the Spirit. If you have love, you will automatically have goodness, meekness, gentleness, etc., and if you have faith, that will produce peace and joy. We were also seeking to cultivate is a good conscience, one "without offense toward God and men" (Acts 24:16). The human heart is like a vault full of contraband goods. If I break into it, it sends out an alarm. If I don't close the door and leave, I am in danger of being taken away by the law and punished.

As each of us opens the door of our hearts, we find all sorts of treasures that delight our sinful souls. Jesus said that "out of the heart proceed evil thoughts"—adulteries, thefts, covetousness, etc. (Mark 7:21–23). But as we begin to take hold of the illegal goods, our conscience will send out an alarm, and if we don't heed the warning and close the door, the Law will eventually come and punish us.

As the Law is applied to the conscience, it opens the seared conscience of the sinner. It also benefits the Christian by keeping the conscience soft and tender before God. If you teach your children that lust and adultery are considered the same thing in the sight of God, it will give them a tender conscience that will send out an alarm when there is temptation.

I frequently receive letters that read something like this: "Johnny gave his heart to Jesus when he was four, but now that he's grown up, he's on drugs and living with his girlfriend."

UNLESS THERE IS REPENTANCE, THERE IS NO SALVATION.

Sue and I weren't seeking a "decision" from our children. Decisions are easy to get. All you have to do is gather a group of children and ask, "Kids, how do you live forever?" "By giving your heart to Jesus!" "Who wants to give their heart to Jesus?" A forest of hands wave. Fifty decisions. The problem is that they will be fine until teen-age temptation reveals their unconverted condition. All we are doing is giving the children and ourselves a false sense of assurance. There must be an understanding of sin, righteousness, and judgment before someone can be saved. Unless there is repentance, there is no salvation. Eternal life comes from "repentance toward God and faith toward our Lord Jesus Christ" (Acts 20:21).

The Phone Bird

The South Island of New Zealand doesn't have crows or mockingbirds. For the first year or so in the U.S., we were fascinated by the different birdcalls we heard in California. One day, while digging a hole, I stopped to listen to the variety of songs. One in particular gripped my ears. It sounded very similar to a phone ringing. I stood there captivated by the sound. It was so close to the sound of a telephone ringing that I thought, *I bet Californians call it a "phone bird." It sounds exactly like a phone ringing.*

Suddenly it dawned on me. It *was* the phone ringing! I missed the caller.

Notice that it was only when my understanding was right that the result was action. The night of my conversion, when my understanding was right, the result was action. My realization that I had sinned against a holy God led me to repent and place my faith in Jesus. "Faith comes by hearing [i.e., a right belief or understanding], and hearing by the word of God" (Romans 10:17). I know a lady who reads her Bible aloud because she believes that faith comes by literally hearing. However, I think it means more than that. As our children heard the Word of God—and as they understood God's holiness, His justice, His truth, His righteousness, His love, and His faithfulness—they acted upon the Word by exercising saving faith, and came to know the salvation of God.

These are the solid rocks with which we should build the family altar: pray; open the Scriptures; place the Law in the heart; involve the senses; liberally use anecdotes; use repetition; share personal stories; and plow on through the "ice age."

Now, commit yourself to having a family altar with your children. If you don't have children of your own, ask God to help you find some, and teach them the Holy Scriptures. Do it as "a living sacrifice, holy, acceptable to God, which is your reasonable service" (Romans 12:1).

Chapter Twenty

TAMPERING WITH THE RECIPE

W HEN I WAS a new Christian, I often quoted statistics about Christian marriages to prove the validity of the claims of Christianity. I would point to the fact that three out of every five U.S. marriages ended in divorce, while only one in every 1,100 ended in divorce in Christian circles. God's love bound a husband and wife together. However, nowadays secular and Christian divorce statistics run hand in hand. For that reason, in this chapter we will take a brief look at what makes a good Christian marriage, because if there is one thing that will throw a child headlong into the path of sin, it's being the byproduct of a bad marriage.

What Is Marriage?

According to the dictionary's cold definition, a marriage is "a legal contract entered into by a man and a woman to live together as husband and wife." Much has been said about the institution, both good and bad. A police officer once stopped a motorist and informed him that his wife had fallen out of the vehicle a mile back. "Good!" exclaimed the motorist. "I thought I'd gone deaf!" Solomon adds his experiential wisdom: "Better to dwell in the wilderness, than with a contentious and angry woman" (Proverbs 21:19). In Luke 14:16–20, when Jesus spoke of individuals being invited to a feast, there seems to be a little dry humor present. The first man's excuse was that he had bought some ground, and then he gave details of why he couldn't come. The second had purchased oxen, and he gave details regarding his excuse. The third merely said, "I have married a wife, and therefore I cannot come."

If wives seem to pick on husbands, it's often because men deserve it. I'm sure that if you are a married woman, you know that men have to be told something twice before it sinks in. You may have also noticed that when God spoke to men in the Bible, He called their name twice: "Abraham, Abraham," "Moses, Moses," "Samuel, Samuel," "Saul, Saul."

Peanut Blackies

Years ago, when our children were small, the moment Sue walked out of the door to attend a mid-week Bible study, I would grab a recipe book to do some experimental baking. On such occasions, I would often tamper with the recipe. My kids and I once made a gingerbread man and woman into which I put double the suggested amount of baking powder.

As we watched through the glass oven door, both the gingerbread man and woman suddenly became puffed up then burst and merged into each other.

How often in the warmth of God's blessings we can exalt ourselves and become puffed up with pride. But if we are truly in Christ, when the intense heat of tribulation comes to us we are suddenly bought back down to earth. Under that heat we merge as one flesh.

Other cooking sprees weren't so spiritual—from unexpected rock cakes to peanut blackies. Sadly, because certain ingredients are missing, many Christians have a "half-baked" marriage. It never rises to their expectations or it crumbles in their hands. Such experiences leave a bad taste in the mouths of all concerned. So, I would like to share with you seven ingredients for a good marriage.

First, establish a regular prayer life *together*. In 1 Peter 3:7 the Bible says, "Likewise, you husbands, dwell with them with understanding, giving honor to the wife, as to the weaker vessel, and as being heirs together of the grace of life, that your prayers may not be hindered." Husbands and wives aren't specifically instructed to pray together. It is taken for granted that we do.

If you are in a high-rise building and there's a fire, the correct response is to drop to your knees. Because smoke rises, you will see more clearly from that position and will avoid the poisonous fumes. Make your prayer-life so second nature to you both that the moment you find yourself in the fires of tribulation, you will drop to your knees. You will see more on the knees of prayer than through the thick and confusing smoke of misfortune.

> AIM TO RID YOURSELF OF A SELFISH AND SINFUL HUMAN NATURE.

Don't say, "I don't know how to pray." Say instead, "I can do all things through Christ who strengthens me" (Philippians 4:13). Then enter His gates with thanksgiving and go into His courts with praise. Thank God for giving you a faithful partner, a home, life, freedom, health, salvation, etc.

Second, aim to rid yourself of a selfish and sinful human nature: "The sacrifices of God are a broken spirit, a broken and a contrite heart" (Psalm 51:17). A broken spirit is found in one who is no longer living for himself. He responds to the pull of the Master's reins. I've counseled enough marriages to know what causes all breakups: it is simply a philosophy of "Not your will, but mine be done." Having a broken spirit means giving up your rights for the rights of your partner.

Don't be like the wife who said to her marriage counselor: "It all started on our wedding day—when he wanted to be in the marriage photos!" Memorize—and put into practice—Philippians 2:3: "Let nothing be done through selfish ambition or conceit, but in lowliness of mind let each esteem others better than himself."

Third, demonstrate grace toward each other. Both parties must come to understand the truth that "we do not wrestle against flesh and blood," but against demonic forces (Ephesians 6:12). Satan's desire is to destroy your marriage (see John 10:10). So in light of that truth, we need to make certain resolutions:

- Never mention the word "divorce" during an argument. The word should shock Christians. The more it is used as an argumentative weapon, the less distasteful it will seem. Avoid statements such as, "Sometimes I can really understand why some marriages end in divorce." If you both resolve that divorce is never an option, you will be motivated to work harder at having a good marriage.

- Vow not to let your emotions lead you to say things you will regret. You are most vulnerable to the one you confide in most—spouses know how to hurt each other. If you feel unable to restrain your sharp tongue in an argument, wait until you have cooled off and can talk reasonably.

- Learn how to say, "I'm sorry." Often I say I'm sorry not because I think I was in the wrong, but because the argument started in the first place. A wife testified at the closing of divorce proceedings, "It all started when he walked out and slammed the door." The husband butted in, "I didn't slam the door!" It was discovered that the wind had caught it. If only faith and humility had been there the day that happened, rather than presumption and pride.

- Be aware of your own faults. Remember the proverb, "All the ways of a man are pure in his own eyes" (16:2). The husband who says, "I have never made a mistake" has a wife who made one big one.

- Agree never to argue in front of your children. You will lose their respect, cause them to question the security of their home, and ruin your witness in front of those most important to you.

- Don't let the sun go down on your anger. Don't "sleep on it," because it will fester and eventually poison you.

Fourth, feed on the Word: "Desire the pure milk of the word, that you might grow thereby" (1 Peter 2:2). Psalm 1 promises God's blessing on all those who meditate on the Law of the Lord "day and night." Both Sue and I have ordered our lives so that we get three meals a day:

- We read the Word in the morning.

- We have evening devotions.

- We read together before we go to sleep.

So many Christians are suffering from spiritual malnutrition. Because they are weak spiritually, the devil is stomping all over them, as is evidenced by the numerous shipwrecked marriages.

Fifth, show love and respect toward each other. Rid yourself of secular prejudice. For instance, those with the "Women's Liberation" mentality believe that the biblical husband-wife relationship is one of a master and a well-trained dog. They couldn't be further from the truth. The Bible does speak of women as the "weaker vessel," which is true physically. However, the biblical order is: as a strong, thorny stem upholds the tender, easily bruised, sweet-smelling rose, so should the husband uphold, love, and respect his wife. When you study a rose, notice how the leaves reach from the stem and embrace the delicate flower. So the arms of the husband should embrace his wife. That is God's order.

The Bible commands husbands, "Love your wives, just as Christ also loved the church and gave Himself for her" (Ephesians 5:25). Men will obey this only to the extent that they understand how much Christ loved the Church. I once spoke at a men's camp to about eighty men, and told them that if they treated their wives sacrificially like this, they would no doubt be rewarded by their wives in a way that all men enjoy. For the next several seconds, you could have heard a pin drop. Suddenly one man, voicing the thought of the entire group, hollered, "Alright!" The room erupted with spontaneous joy, laughter, and loud amens.

> WE ENTER THE KINGDOM OF GOD THROUGH THE HEAT OF "MANY TRIBULATIONS."

Ladies, if your husband doesn't open the car door for you when you get home at night, stay in the car until he does. If, however, you see the bedroom light switch off, give up and try again another time. Husbands, if you know what's good for you, show respect for your wife. It *will* become mutual, and you will be rewarded. You will reap what you sow, and thus enrich and lift your marriage.

Sixth, communicate. The Bible says that when a man and woman are joined in marriage, they "become one flesh." Sue and I met while we were working in a bank. At work we were called "the budgies" because we used to sit together each day and I would peck at her lunch. Nothing has changed. Not only is Sue my wife, but she's my best friend.

Here's a strange thing. In Acts 17:21, we are told that the

Athenians and strangers did nothing else but "to tell or to hear some new thing." What? Grown men sitting around like elderly ladies in a knitting circle, yapping about new things? *That's almost unbelievable.* Yet their appetite isn't to be compared to modern man's insatiable appetite to hear of new things. We have huge publications nearly three feet wide and two feet high, packed full of new things. They are called "newspapers"—and there are thousands of them. Telling about new things is a multibillion-dollar industry. We have radio news, prime-time TV news, early morning news, late evening news, and even "breaking news"!

Think on this sobering thought, husbands. If the mute button worked on your wife as well as it does on the TV, and she was talking during the news, at which one would you aim the remote? You will always have news to listen to, so don't take for granted that you will always have your wife to keep you company. Communication is the glue that keeps the marriage bond strong.

Lastly, expect trials. There is no avoiding them. The Bible warns us that we enter the kingdom of God through the heat of "many tribulations." The heat will show us whether we have the correct ingredients. It will "perfect, establish, strengthen, and settle you" (1 Peter 5:10). So make sure you are genuine in your faith. Try always to live with a conscience "without offense" toward both God and man, and you will never fail.

Chapter Twenty-One

IF THE AVERAGE GIRL KNEW

A SCIENTIST ONCE conducted an interesting series of experiments. He placed two people in separate rooms, facing each other through a sheet of glass. Each person had a row of lights at his or her fingertips. As a light came on, they raced to switch it off. The person who turned the light off first won. The winner then sent an electric shock into the opponent. The interesting thing was that the winner was able to choose the degree of shock sent, on a one-to-ten scale.

The scientist found that, without exception, alcohol affected the size of the shocks that the volunteers sent. When the volunteers were sober, they always sent less-powerful shocks. But when they were intoxicated—regardless of whether they were male or female—they became very cruel, sending the opponent a far greater shock.

Even though the drug would seem to make people jolly, when they are threatened in any way, most drunks become very aggressive. The conclusion was that human nature is actually very volcanic. The nicest of us has the potential to blow our tops off, if someone scratches our surface. The learned scientist could have saved himself a lot of trouble if he had taken the time to read the Bible. It says that the heart of man is "deceitfully wicked."

A concerned young Christian showed me a letter recently to get my opinion. It was from a very upset person who thought that she might have homosexual tendencies. Society has been hoodwinked into accepting many lies, and one of the greatest is that homosexuals are "born that way." If that is true, we were all born homosexuals. As we developed, we all had the capacity to be a homosexual. As I grew, I found that I had the potential to be a rapist, a murderer, a thief, a liar, and an adulterer. In fact, as I searched deeply into my own heart I found the capacity to get into all sorts of perversions. All I discovered was a sin-filled heart.

Becoming a Christian doesn't mean that you will now live a life of purity. In fact, now more than ever, you will be increasingly conscious of your moral behavior, and sin will seem to be more evident. Whereas before you would get angry and hardly give it a second thought, now it will grieve you when you sin.

I have spoken with hundreds of Christians who are often at a point of tears because they find themselves burning in a battle with sexual lust. Take consolation, dear Christian— you are not alone. One sign that you are a Christian is that you will be *battling* with sin. If you are not fighting sin, it's probably because you have surrendered to it, or perhaps you have never even come across from the enemy's side. Don't think that the battle will become easier as you get older. I have counseled many a mature Christian (including a seventy-four-year-old man) who was battling a problem of lust.

If you are a woman, dress modestly. If the average girl knew how the average guy thought, she would dress with a little more discretion. The length of some Christian girls' dresses reveals their naiveté. Girls, get this straight—there are only two sorts of men: depraved and depraved who are forgiven. Show me a normal man (outside of Jesus Christ) who says he has never lusted, and I will show you a liar.

If you are a Christian and you have a problem with pornography, the following ten principles may help you:

- Why don't you take some pornography to church and look at it during worship? You may as well, because God is just as present in your bedroom as He is in the church building.

- Face the fact that you may not be saved. Examine yourself to ensure that Christ is living in you (2 Corinthians 13:5). See Romans 6:11–22; 8:1–14; Ephesians 5:3–8.

- Realize that when you give yourself to pornography, you are committing adultery (Matthew 5:27,28).

- Grasp the serious nature of your sin. Jesus said that it would be better for you to be blind and go to heaven, than for your eye to cause you to sin and end up in hell (Matthew 5:29).

- Those who profess to be Christians yet give themselves to pornographic material evidently lack the fear of God (Proverbs 16:6). Cultivate the fear of God by reading Proverbs 2:1–5.

- Read Psalm 51 and make it your own prayer.

- Memorize James 1:14,15 and 1 Corinthians 10:13. Follow Jesus' example (Matthew 4:3–11) and quote the Word of God when you are tempted.

- Make no provision for your flesh (Romans 13:14; 1 Peter 2:11). Get rid of every access to pornographic material— the Internet, printed literature, TV, videos, and movies. Stop feeding the fire.

- Guard your heart with all diligence (Proverbs 4:23). Don't let the demonic realm have access to your thought-life. If you give yourself to it, you will become its slave (Romans 6:16). Read the Bible daily, without fail. As you submit to

God, the devil will flee (James 4:7,8).

- The next time temptation comes, do fifty push-ups, then fifty sit-ups. If you are still burning, repeat the process (see 1 Corinthians 9:27).

Diving or Falling

During a World Cup soccer tournament some years ago, I saw a player trip right in front of the goalmouth. I was certain he would be awarded a penalty, but the referee waved the play on. The player did a "Hollywood," or according to the referee, he "took a dive." The commentator agreed. If he had been tripped, he was innocent and should be compensated. But if it was deliberate, and he did take a dive, he was deceitful and should himself have been penalized.

His motive was what determined his guilt or innocence. Therein lies the difference between the hypocrite (a pretend Christian) and the genuine Christian. The hypocrite *dives* into sin, while the Christian *falls*. One is guilty and will receive the ultimate penalty, while the other is innocent. The Epistle of John contains a very comforting Scripture: "Now by this we know that we know Him, if we keep His commandments." How do I know that I know the Lord? Because for twenty-two years I couldn't have cared less about God; now, after my conversion, I have a burning desire to live for His will and honor. Nothing matters more to me than to please God. I have been given a "new heart" with new desires. Something in me *wants* to keep His Commandments. That's how I know that I know Him. When I sin, it is against my will. If I take the biggest piece of chocolate cake, suddenly I feel grieved. I don't want to be greedy. I want to be kind, caring and loving. If I sin, it's because I "fall," not because I "dive."

This is the clear teaching of Scripture: "Whoever has been

born of God does not sin…" (1 John 3:9). If you dive into sin, if you deliberately plan to do something you know is wrong, you are in big trouble. You may be a false convert: "If we say that we have fellowship with Him, and walk in darkness, we lie and do not practice the truth."

Some time ago, I was speaking in Houston, Texas. The Christians who had invited me to speak had warmly welcomed me into their huge nine-bedroom home. My warm feelings at their reception cooled a little when they told me that they had caught seven scorpions in the house during the previous week. I am not a great fan of scorpions or spiders. Once as Sue and I walked into a bedroom in Hawaii, she said, "Don't look now, but there is a spider on the wall!" There was. Right above my side of the bed was a huge black beast about the size of a man's fist. It was so big, we could hear the sounds of its feet as it walked across the wall.

> THE HYPOCRITE *DIVES* INTO SIN, WHILE THE CHRISTIAN *FALLS.*

I crept across to the other side of the room, grabbed the fly spray, and sprayed the monster. Suddenly it sprung off the wall onto our bed and disappeared! If we couldn't locate it, there was no way we were going to sleep in that room. When it appeared from under the bed, I aimed the spray and fired. I think the creature drowned, rather than dying from asphyxiation.

So I wasn't exactly excited at the thought of scorpions. In fact, I thought I saw one while I was speaking at the church that Sunday morning. I pointed at the carpet about fifteen feet in front of me and screamed out, "Scorpion!" right in the middle of the sermon. It turned out to be a large grasshopper, much to the delight of the congregation.

On Sunday evening, I was in the middle of delivering my message when I looked down at the pulpit and saw a black spider heading toward my hand. It looked like a small tarantula so I screamed, "Tarantula!" Then I picked up a large cup of water that was on the pulpit and poured it on the spider. Afterwards, a woman told me that she had to keep thumping her husband because he was still shaking with laughter twenty minutes later.

It wasn't a tarantula as I thought. It was just a black widow, America's most deadly spider.

Listen carefully. If you are going to be totally sold out to God, there is going to be an ugly beast that wants to get his teeth into your flesh. When the Bible speaks of the flesh, it is referring to your sinful nature. When the demon of lust knocks on the door, don't answer it. Tip the water of the Word on its hideous head. That's what Jesus did when the devil tempted Him. He quoted the Scriptures at him, something he doesn't like at all. The effect is like shining a bright light on an ugly cockroach.

Last Words

I will never forget an experience I had while ministering in Australia. During a service, an elderly man in his mid-eighties stood up and (uninvited) made his way to the pulpit. The poor man was all skin and bones. With trembling hands, and voice quaking with conviction, he said, "I have only one thing to say, and that is when I was a young man I gave myself to sport." He hardly needed to say any more. Where was his physique, where was his muscle, where was the glory? *Listen to his wisdom.* Don't waste yourself on the vanities of this life. The only difference between you and the elderly is time. Now, while you are able to move and to speak, give yourself to that which is eternal. I'm not saying to neglect physical health, but to give thought to your priorities. Everything you attain outside of the kingdom of God will eventually be torn from your hands by death. It would do every Christian a great deal of good to read a book called *Last Words of Saints and Sinners* by Herbert Lockyer. It's not the sort of book you read from cover to cover, but a few moments browsing its pages tends to get the point across. Let me quote a few last words.

When Louis XVII, the King of France, died in 1795, his final words were, "I have something to tell you!" He was either a very dry practical joker, a sadist, or one who learned the hard way that death waits for no man.

General John Sedwick's memorable last words were spoken during a battle in 1864. As he looked over a barricade, he boldly declared, "Stand up, you cowards—they couldn't hit an elephant at this dist—!" The brilliant Albert Einstein stated some last words, but no one knows what they were. Astute though he was, Einstein made the mistake of uttering them in his native German tongue, which his nurse didn't understand.

Those who neglect the salvation of God reveal their foolishness by their last words. John Randolph, an American statesman of the last century, cried, "Remorse, remorse, remorse! Let me see the word. Show me it in a dictionary. Write it down. Ah! Remorse, you don't know what it means. I cast myself on the Lord Jesus Christ for mercy!"

Millions who reject the gospel sink into death in silent terror. Others who trust in Jesus understand the parting words of famous poet John Milton: "Death is the great key that opens the palace of eternity."

It is my hope that if you and I do have any last words, they will be in the spirit of the final words of Jesus (before He died). His cry on the cross was, "It is finished!" (John 19:30).

In other words, He completely accomplished what He set out to do—the will of God. Yet these weren't really His last words. After He burst from the grave, He said many things. His last recorded words (after He died and was resurrected) were to the apostle John: "Surely I am coming quickly" (Revelation 22:20).

If we die before He returns, we too will triumph over death. Our faith in Him will hold back the terrors of death. The more you cultivate faith in God, the less fear will have entry. If, however, we are alive when the sky rolls back to reveal His unspeakable glory, we will be transformed from these bodies of death into incorruptible bodies. We will never again experience pain, fear, loneliness, suffering, aging, or death. Meditate on the marvels of the human body and this fantastic creation God has given to us. Think of the beauty of the rain forests of the Amazon, the glory of a sunset, the grandeur of the Swiss Alps, and the magnificence of the Grand Canyon. Then remind yourself that this is all under God's curse, that it's a fallen creation. It is nothing but a faint shadow of the "new heavens and the new earth." The Bible tells us that our eyes have never seen, nor our ears heard, nor has it ever entered into our imaginations, the wonderful things God has in store for those who love Him.

TOO MANY CHRISTIANS ARE IGNORANT OF THEIR HOPE IN CHRIST.

Too many Christians are ignorant of their hope in Christ. They have little understanding of what God has for those who obey His Word. God's kingdom is coming to this earth: Jesus taught us to pray, "Your kingdom come. Your will be done on earth as it is in heaven" (Matthew 6:10). This old earth is going to have the curse removed, and God's blessing will dwell upon it. When Jesus took the crown of thorns upon His head, He was taking the Genesis curse upon Himself. The starving children, the snake bites, shark attacks, scorpion bites, pestilence, earthquakes, cancers, floods, hurricanes, tornadoes, and the seemingly endless sufferings of humanity are all results of the curse—they are not God's perfect will. The Bible tells us that He "gives us richly all things to enjoy" (1 Timothy 6:17). But these promised "pleasures forevermore" are only for those who obey Him and trust in Jesus Christ.

I once read of a young man who jumped from a plane for his first skydive. When he pulled his main parachute, it failed to open. As he thought about what he was supposed to do regarding the emergency parachute, he hit the ground. His friends rushed up to him, thinking he was dead. They instead found that he had miraculously landed on freshly plowed ground and was still alive. As he lay there with fourteen broken bones, and a bone protruding vertically from his leg, he mumbled, "Boy, did I blow it!"

He was right; he blew it. He had listened to his instructor. He had believed. However, he hadn't obeyed. *Don't blow it for eternity.* Listen, believe, and obey. Obey not only the gospel—to repent and trust in Jesus—but also the Great Commission Jesus gave to each believer—to go out and share the gospel with others.

Pray that God gives you great wisdom and boldness, and then pursue those who are in the shadow of death. If you don't witness for your faith, neither will you pray with passion for the lost. Your guilt will keep you from praying for laborers because you will feel like a hypocrite if you are not a laborer yourself. The devil has a double victory, because you will pray for everything except what Jesus told us to pray for.

If you are fearful about witnessing, begin by using gospel

tracts. Don't try to talk to people, just put the literature in different public places. Crawl before you walk. The time will come when God will so burden you that compassion will swallow your fears. I know of one man who received 1,700 letters of salvation from people who made a commitment to Christ from a tract he had published.

Sue and I were once sitting in a doctor's waiting room. It was an ideal place to give out tracts, but as usual, I thought of a hundred reasons why I shouldn't. First, I didn't want to embarrass her by walking around the room giving out Christian literature. Second, most were reading and the last thing on their minds was God. Third, I was always giving out tracts, so today I was going to have a break, etc.

> GOD WILL SO BURDEN YOU THAT COMPASSION WILL SWALLOW YOUR FEARS.

Suddenly a three-year-old girl right in front of us began to recite the Lord's Prayer out loud. Then she started over again. Then again, this time louder. Everyone in the waiting room could hear her. By now, they were all thinking about God, whether they wanted to or not. The fourth time she started, it was even louder. That's when I gave in and handed out the tracts.

You are not alone in your fears. Since I became a Christian in 1972, I have given out approximately 200,000 tracts, and yet I still battle with fear. But that doesn't stop me. I always have tracts, and if God helps me, I will continue to give them out (if you ever find me in public without tracts, I will give you $1,000).

A tract written by an atheist dramatically changed the life of C. T. Studd (1860–1931). It helped him turn from luke-warm Christianity to being on fire for God. After reading the tract, he walked away from great financial wealth and status as one of the greatest athletes in England's history to become a missionary in China and Africa. Here is the tract:

> Did I firmly believe, as millions say they do, that the knowledge and practice of religion in this life influences destiny in another, religion would mean to me everything. I would cast away all earthly enjoyments as dross, earthly cares as follies, and earthly thoughts and feelings as vanity. Religion would be my first waking thought, and my last image before sleep sank me into unconsciousness. I should labor in its cause alone. I would take thought for the tomorrow of eternity alone. I would esteem one soul gained for heaven worth a life of suffering. Earthly consequences should never stay my hand, nor seal my lips. Earth, its joys and its griefs, would occupy no moment of my thoughts. I would strive to look upon eternity alone, and on the immortal souls around me, soon to be everlastingly happy or everlastingly miserable. I would go forth to the world and preach it in season and out of season and my text would be: "What shall it profit a man if he gain the whole world and lose his own soul?"

Mr. Studd said, "I at once saw that this was truly the consistent Christian life. When I looked back upon my own life I saw how inconsistent it had been. I therefore determined that from that time forth my life should be consistent, and I set myself to know what was God's will for me. But this time I determined not to consult with flesh and blood, but just wait until God should show me." C. T. Studd lived his motto: "Some wish to live within the sound of church or chapel bell; I want to run a rescue shop within a yard of hell."

May God give each of us the love and courage to, by any means, firmly hold passengers out the door by their ankles until they see the seriousness of their plight. Then we will have the joy of telling them of the love of God displayed at Calvary, giving them that glorious parachute that can save them from sure death.

Trial by Fire

Peter warmed his cold hands by the fire. He had declared that he would *never* be ashamed of Jesus. Yet he was about to deny Him—to a maid. He would soon go through a fiery trial, and three times be found guilty of being ashamed of the one he called his Lord.

Peter made a number of mistakes that dark night. Instead of praying to avoid temptation, as Jesus had told him to do, he slept while Jesus prayed (Luke 22:45). He missed his Gethsemane experience, and when the hour of temptation came upon him, in one sense he was still asleep. It would take the loud crowing of a rooster to awaken him. He also resorted to violence in the face of the adversity (Luke 22:49–51).

He was supposed to be a follower of Jesus, a fisher of men, but he followed Him "at a distance." Peter seated himself in the midst of the ungodly (Luke 22:55) without any thought for their eternal well-being. He didn't want to rock the boat by casting out any nets.

Scripture tells us that a servant girl saw him as he sat by the fire. She was sure that she had seen him with Jesus, but Peter adamantly denied it, saying, "Woman, I do not know Him." Two more accusers, then two more denials. The accusations came out of the mouths of three witnesses. The trial by fire was over. He was three times guilty.

When Peter remembered what Jesus had said, he went out and wept *bitterly* (Luke 22:62). Like Isaiah, he had already lamented over his own sinfulness when he once fell at the feet of Jesus and said, "Depart from me, for I am a sinful man, O Lord!" *But this experience was different.*

Peter's denial at first seems a mystery. For three years he had unashamedly walked with Jesus of Nazareth. He had even stayed by His side when he knew that the Jews sought to kill Him (see John 11:8). *How then could Peter be afraid of a servant?* He stepped out of the boat to walk on water. He had boldly risked his life by taking his sword in his hand in defense of the Lord. He was no wimp. No, his fear was not simply because he knew Jesus. It was something deeper.

It would seem that the Roman cross was what Peter feared. This instrument of punishment was no mere lethal injection. It was cruel and *usual* punishment, which the Romans used the cross to execute lawbreakers. They had raised the crossbar of human suffering to a higher level.

The cross was *intended* to cause fear. Its grizzly public display was a freeway billboard, designed to deter the busy traffic of crime. Peter had no doubt seen men writhe like worms, as barbed Roman steel penetrated their tender flesh. He had seen soldiers dutifully hold down unwilling and grasping hands. He had heard the unforgettable thud of the hammer as it pushed cold nails through warm human flesh, releasing gushes of blood from hands and feet. He had been a silent witness as hardened men suddenly became screaming animals, horrified by the stark reality of their terrible plight. One look into their eyes was enough to terrorize the most callous of human hearts.

He had also watched the unspeakable torture as the cross was heartlessly dropped into the ground, ripping apart mortal flesh like a great beast viciously tearing its helpless prey. Perhaps it wasn't the servant he feared. Perhaps it was the terrifying threat of the Roman torture stake.

Peter had once before revealed his disdain of the cross, bringing the sharpest of rebukes from the Savior (see Mark

8:31–33). Jesus had cited Peter's motive (even then) as a case of "not Your will, but mine be done."

You Are Not Ashamed

Perhaps you too once dropped to your knees at the feet of the Son of God and confessed your sins. You know what it is to lament over your wicked heart. Now you belong to Jesus ... and you are *not* ashamed to confess Him before men.

Let me therefore ask you a few probing questions. It's a cold night. Come closer to the fire so that you can warm your hands. Come nearer to the light so that we can see your face. Let's see how cold you are. When did you last share your faith? I'm not asking if you have a "God is good" sticker on your car, or if you wear a "fish" badge. I'm not asking whether you are ashamed to say that you belong to Jesus. Of course you're not. I'm asking when you last shared the *bloodied* cross. When did you last preach Christ *crucified?* When did you last *plead* with a sinner to flee from God's wrath and to shelter in the cross?

Perhaps you have been following Jesus, but you've dropped back just a little ... because of the cross. Any mention of its bloodstained frame will mean that a sinful world will stop smiling at your walk with Jesus. It will instead begin to spit out its hatred. You are afraid of what the apostle Paul called the "offense of the cross." Like Peter, you dread it because of the personal pain it would bring.

Perhaps this is because you have been sleeping when you should have been praying, "Not my will, but Yours be done." You have missed your Gethsemane experience. Consequently your fear of the cross has kept you back from where you should be—you are following Jesus "at a distance."

Are you guilty of denying your Lord? Do you hear the crowing of conscience? Has its voice awakened you? Perhaps you need to go somewhere and weep *bitterly*.

We know that it was the Holy Spirit that gave Peter his boldness on the Day of Pentecost. Possibly it was his bitter weeping that put him head and shoulders above the rest on that day. The other disciples were filled with the same Holy Spirit. The other disciples heard the rushing mighty wind. They had the same fire above their heads, but it was Peter who stood up with a holy fire in his tongue.

We need more Christians like Peter—those who will stand up and unashamedly preach the blood of the cross. We need more who have resigned themselves to daily take up the cross and follow Jesus. They have willingly yielded their hands and their feet to the painful and penetrating nails of persecution. Their Gethsemane experience has given them the sober truth that if their blood must fall on the soil of this world for the sake of the gospel, so be it.

We need those whose concern is only heaven's mandate, not their own will—those who have a deep concern for the welfare of a hell-bound world—a world whose punishment will not be merely a Roman cross. Oswald J. Smith said, "Oh, to realize that souls, precious, never dying souls, are perishing all around us, going out into the blackness of darkness and despair, eternally lost, and yet to feel no anguish, shed no tears, know no travail! How little we know of the compassion of Jesus!"

May God help us to understand that those who die in their sins fall into the hands of the Living God, and the Bible says that is a *fearful* thing. They will not have the option to welcome the embrace of death to bring relief from their terrible torture.

Be True to Yourself

If you have made it through this publication and you still

don't have peace with God, then your blood will be upon your own head. On Judgment Day, I will be free from your blood. I have poured out my heart to you. I have reasoned with you. I have pleaded with you—and you will have no one to blame but yourself for refusing to receive God's forgiveness. If you won't be convinced of sin this side of the grave, then it will take hell to convince you on the other side. Then you will know the full meaning of the word "remorse." Harsh though these words may seem, God knows my motivation is one of love and concern for you.

The word "atheist" is composed of two Greek words: *a* (without) and *theos* (God). By your own choice you are without God, and consequently without hope.

At least be true to yourself and drop your "atheist" label. You are just using the word as a very weak and transparent shield for sin. The knowledge you now have makes you guiltier than you were before you read this book. Your parachute is full of holes. Dwight Eisenhower said,

> It takes no brains to be an atheist. Any stupid person can deny the existence of a supernatural power because man's physical senses cannot detect it. But there cannot be ignored the influence of conscience, the respect we feel for the Moral Law, the mystery of first life...or the marvelous order in which the universe moves about us on this earth. All these evidence the handiwork of the beneficent Deity...That Deity is the God of the Bible and of Jesus Christ, His Son.

You can no longer be a believer in the religion of atheism. You now know there is a God. Your faith has been shattered. You don't even believe you are an atheist. I certainly don't; neither does God. He calls you a fool. I tend to agree: "The fool has said in his heart, 'There is no God'" (Psalm 14:1).

REASONING FOR THE FAITH

T HE FOLLOWING questions are taken from the web site of a Hollywood atheist organization. As they have stated, this information is useful for those who "haven't thought much about religion since childhood and want to test their faith with adult questions... These questions are worthwhile only to those who think reason is the most valid tool in forming opinions."

I have given answers to their difficulties. Perhaps these answers will help you with any questions you may still have about Christianity.

1) How would you define God, and why are you so convinced that there is one?

God is the Creator, Upholder, and the Sustainer of the universe. He revealed Himself to Moses as the one and only true God.

2) If everything needs a creator, then who or what created God?

He created "time," and because we dwell in the dimension of time *reason* demands that all things have a beginning and an end. God, however, dwells outside of the dimension of time. He moves through time as we flip through the pages of a history book; this can be proven by simple study of the prophecies of Matthew 24, Luke 21, and 2 Timothy 3. He dwells in "eternity," having no beginning or end. This is a dimension in which all humanity will dwell when God withdraws time.

3) How can something that cannot be described be said to exist?
The color blue cannot be accurately described to a man who was born blind. Just because it cannot be described doesn't mean that it doesn't exist. There is plant life on the bottoms of the deepest oceans that have never been seen by man, let alone described by him. Despite this, they still exist. Does the (unseen) far side of a planet fail to exist merely because man cannot describe it?

4) Since there are countless religions in the world today claiming to be the one true religion, *why do you think yours is truer than theirs?*
No religion is "truer" than another. "Religion" is man's futile effort to try to find peace with God. The Christian doesn't strive to have peace with his Creator. It was given to him in the person of the Savior. The uniqueness of Jesus of Nazareth is His statement, "The Son of Man has power on earth to forgive sins." No religion of man can do that. Christianity is not a manmade "religion," but a personal relationship with the one true God.

5) Can more than one of these religions be right?
In one sweeping statement, Jesus discards all other religions as a means of finding forgiveness of sins. Jesus, who claimed to be God, said, "I am the way, the truth, and the life. No one comes to the Father except through Me" (John 14:6). The Bible says about Jesus, "There is one God and one Mediator between God and men, the Man Christ Jesus" (1 Timothy 2:5) and, "Nor is there salvation in any other, for there is no other name under heaven given among men by which we must be saved" (Acts 4:12). See also Answer #4.

6) *If you feel* in your heart *that your religion is the right one, how do you answer those of other faiths who claim the same thing?*

Christians don't base their faith on feelings; their feelings are irrelevant to truth. If I am flying from Los Angeles to New York, my feelings about whether I am going in the right direction have nothing to do with that fact. We can *know* with our intellect that Christianity is true, regardless of our feelings. The Bible's thousands of fulfilled prophecies, historical accuracy, and many infallible proofs attest to its reliability.

7) *How do you settle the debate and find out which of these religions, if any, is the right one?*

Jesus promises that He and the Father will reveal themselves to all who love and obey Him. This is the ultimate challenge to any skeptic. If you repent and place your faith in Jesus Christ, He will give you eternal life and you can *know* that your eternity is secure.

8) *Why does God allow all these false religions to exist?*

Because God wants mankind to worship and love Him, He gave Adam and Eve the free will to choose whether to obey or disobey Him. Humanity has chosen to reject God's way and instead seeks to establish their own righteousness through works-based religions.

God allows these false religions and atheism to exist for the same reason He allows sinful humans to exist. The Bible tells us that God is not willing that any should perish (regardless of whether they are religious or profess atheism), but that they all come to repentance.

9) *Is the bloody history of Christianity consistent with what is supposed to be a religion of love, or does it simply illustrate the consequences of abandoning reason for faith?*

The Bible commands Christians to love their enemies and do good to those who spitefully use them. The terrorists in the World Trade Center tragedy carried out their agenda in the name of Allah (their god). This is nothing new. The Crusaders and others who have committed atrocities in the name of Christianity were also evil men who were carrying out their depraved agenda. A thinking person can distinguish between those who use the Christian faith for their own political or "religious" ends and those who are true followers of Jesus.

10) *If everything is the product of a "grand design" by an omniscient, benevolent designer, why is the history of life a record of horrible suffering, blundering waste, and miserable failures? Why does this God go through billions of years of such carnage without yet arriving at His goal?*

God's original creation was "good," but because of mankind's sin we now live in a "fallen" creation. Before sin entered the world there was no suffering, disease, decay, or death. The Bible's explanation of suffering actually substantiates the truth of Scripture.

11) *Why did God intervene so many times in human affairs during antiquity (according to the Bible) and yet not do anything during the Holocaust of the Second World War?*

No human can claim to know whether or not God intervened in the affairs of humanity at any time between 1939 and 1945. However, the Old Testament makes it very clear that there were times when God didn't intervene in the affairs of His people. He purposefully allowed their enemies to overpower them so that they would turn back to Him.

12) Why should one's inner convictions about the existence of God indicate that He/She/They/It exists outside of that person's mind?

The Bible says that God has placed eternity in the hearts of men and given all people everywhere an awareness of Him so that they are without excuse. He created us to know Him. Throughout history and throughout the world, all cultures acknowledge the existence of God.

Besides, why should one's inner convictions about the non-existence of God indicate that He doesn't exist outside of that person's mind? Our personal convictions and beliefs do not affect reality. God simply is.

13) Can a God who would abandon his children when they needed him the most still be considered "all good"?

One of the great errors of humanity is to misunderstand the meaning of "good." A "good" judge will pronounce a stiff sentence on a vicious murderer. A "loving" judge who dismisses a case against a vicious killer because he loves him is not a good judge. Justice and goodness are inseparable. Many times God chastened Israel (gave them their just dessert) *because* of His goodness. He wanted them to turn back to Him for their own good.

14) If something is not rational, should it be believed anyway?

At one time, the concept of a thousand-ton aircraft flying through the air seemed irrational and absurd. But after man studied the laws of physics, it was discovered to be quite rational and believable. If one studies God's Word and understands His Law, Christianity is seen to be infinitely rational and believable. Atheism, on the other hand, rejects logic and evidence and is the epitome of irrationalism. It should be abandoned by any rational person as being foolishness.

15) If the God of the Bible is "all good," why does he himself say that he created evil (Isaiah 45:7)?

The word translated "evil" in that verse ("I make peace, and create evil") actually means "calamity" or "suffering"—God uses both good and bad events in our lives to bring us into a right relationship with Him. However, because God is sovereign over all events, He did allow evil to come into being.

God gave mankind a choice to have a loving relationship with Him. The original sin was when Adam and Eve chose to eat from the tree of knowledge of good and evil. Once man knew both good and evil, he had to choose between the two. Because God wants people to worship Him freely out of love and enjoy His incredible blessings, He tells each one of us: "See, I have set before you today life and good, death and evil…, therefore choose life, that both you and your descendants may live" (Deuteronomy 30:15,19).

16) Is there a better way than reason to acquire knowledge and truth?

No. That's why the Bible says, "'Come now, and let us reason together,' says the LORD." That's why when the apostle Paul spoke "the words of truth and reason," King Agrippa said, "You almost persuade me to become a Christian." That's why Paul "reasoned" with Felix (the governor) about "righteousness, self-control, and judgment to come." And that's why Felix "was afraid."

17) If you would answer #16 with "faith," then why are there so many contradictory faiths in the world?

There are many faiths because all nations recognize that there is a Creator. However, in their ignorance they worship the moon, the sun, or an idol. No one has ever found an atheistic tribe, because they are not that ignorant. God has given light to every man.

18) *If you believe, as many do, that all religions worship the same God under different names, how do you explain the existence of religions which have more than one god, or Buddhism, which, in its pure form, has no god?*

All religions do not worship the same God. People who reject the one true God of the Bible can find any number of gods, of any type, to suit their tastes. They may choose to worship a small wooden god that asks only for shelf space, one that promises paradise in exchange for a certain number of daily prayers, or one that demands specific offerings or good deeds. People who reject the one true God have always been able to devise a replacement.

19) *What would it take to convince you that you are wrong?*

I have already been convinced that I was wrong. I was wrong for my 22 years of unconverted life. Conversion to Christianity is when a fallible human being admits that he is wrong and that the infallible Creator is right.

20) *If nothing can convince you that you are wrong, then why should your faith be considered anything other than a cult?*

A cult is defined as "a system of religious worship and ritual," which would seem to describe every manmade religion. Christianity, on the other hand, is not a strict adherence to ritual, but a personal relationship with a living God. When a person repents of his sin and places his trust in Jesus, God fills him with His Spirit—the person becomes spiritually alive. He has moved out of the realm of *belief* into the realm of *experience*. Once he knows the truth, nothing can convince him otherwise.

Besides, why should adherence to the truth be a determining factor in whether a belief is valid? I believe in gravity and nothing can convince me that I am wrong—but my belief is still true.

21) If an atheist lives a decent, moral life, why should a loving, compassionate God care whether or not we believe in Him/ Her/It?

No matter how decent and moral we think we are, we have all sinned by violating God's holy Laws. To see how you fare against God's standard, review the Ten Commandments (given in Exodus chapter 20). God's concern isn't whether or not we *believe* in Him; the Bible says that even the demons believe—and tremble. God commands that we repent of our sins and trust Jesus Christ alone for our salvation. If we refuse do that, we will be given justice on the Day of Judgment and we will perish.

22) How can the same God who, according to the Old Testament, killed everybody on Earth except for eight people be considered as anything other than evil?

Look at the lifestyle of those people—they deserved death because of their evil actions. That's what happens when men reject God. We will all die because God, the Judge of the universe, has pronounced the death sentence upon us: "The soul who sins shall die." Criminals rarely speak well of the judge. To them, he is "evil."

23) Must we hate our families and ourselves in order to be good Christians? (Luke 14:26)

No. Luke 14:26 is what is known as "hyperbole"—a statement of extremes, contrasting love with hate for emphasis sake. Jesus tells us that the first and greatest Commandment is to love God with all of our heart, soul, and mind (Matthew 22:37,38). As much as we treasure our spouse and family, and even our own life, there should be no one whom we love and value more than God, no one who takes precedence in our life. To place love for another (including ourself) above God is idolatry.

24) Since the ancient world abounded with tales of resurrected Savior-Gods that were supposed to have returned from the dead to save humanity, why is the Jesus myth any more reliable than all the others?

I have never heard of any "tales of resurrected Savior-Gods that were supposed to have returned from the dead to save humanity." Any myths there have been have died out for lack of proof. The "Jesus myth," however, has endured through the ages in cultures all around the world because it is true and provable. Simply go to John 14:21. Read it through a few times and then try it...if you dare. If you place your trust in Jesus Christ for your salvation, He will come into your life and reveal Himself to you.

25) If the Bible is the inerrant word of God, why does it contain so many factual errors, such as the two contradictory accounts of creation in Genesis?

There are not two accounts of creation in Genesis. Chapter 1 gives the account of creation; chapter 2 gives *details* of the same creation. I have been reading the Bible every day for thirty years (without fail) and I am not aware of any "factual errors."

26) Why isn't the Bible written in a straightforward way that leaves no doubt about what it means?

The Bible is *very* clear to those who obey God. It says of itself that it is spiritually understood, and that the "natural" man cannot receive the things of God. To someone who hasn't been born spiritually, "they are foolishness to him; nor can he know them, because they are spiritually discerned" (1

Corinthians 2:14). However, we can all understand enough to realize that we have sinned against a holy God and need to repent. Once we do that, God gives us the ability to understand His Word.

27) The last time Christianity attained total power, it resulted in the Dark Ages, so why should we expect anything different from Christian fundamentalists today?

It was not Christianity but the Roman Catholic church that had power during the Dark Ages. The doctrines of the Roman Catholic church and the teachings of the Bible are opposed to one another. It was the Roman Catholic church that opposed Galileo, was responsible for the Inquisition, and refused the common people access to the Bible during the Dark Ages. The Christian Church isn't seeking "total power." Its agenda is not political.

28) Has anyone ever been killed in the name of atheism?

Yes. Atheistic Communist regimes have slaughtered 100 million people. In China an incredible 72 million were murdered, in the Soviet Union 20 million, Cambodia 2.3 million, North Korea 2 million, Africa 1.7 million, Afghanistan 1.5 million, Vietnam 1 million, Eastern Europe 1 million, Latin America 150,000.

However, the full implications of atheistic belief won't be seen until the Day of Judgment, when those who profess to be atheists and therefore ignore God's mercy will lose their most precious procession, their very life.

END NOTES

1. The Barrier-Comfort debate is available on audio and video from www.raycomfort.com or by calling 800-437-1893.

2. "Each year, 120,000 patients die because of medical error." *Reader's Digest*, June 2000.

3. Some bananas have the three ridges on the near side. This means that the banana is to be held with the curve facing away, so obviously the banana is to be shared.

4. Madalyn Murray O'Hair was tragically murdered by another atheist, David R. Waters. Waters admitted his role in the 1995 kidnapping and murder of O'Hair, her son and granddaughter.

5. Darwin then admitted that he believed such an absurdity.

6. I sent April Pedersen "Atheist's Obstacles" for her thoughts. This was her reply: "Thank you for sending! It's worded with impeccable logic... It's nearly impossible to find holes in your premise that in order to claim there is no God, one must be omniscient. It's impossible for anyone to be omniscient. And you addressed the issue of "unanswered" prayers well too, where God exists independently regardless of our views of prayers, and is independent of the Bible as well... So *that* explains what people are praying to when they pray at ball games and the like... They have created a false god as they want to see him, without even knowing they have fallen into this self-centered trap... an idol..."

7. One favorite argument of professing atheists is that Christians can't use "circular reasoning" by trying to *prove* the Bible by quoting *from* the Bible. The "circular reasoning" argument is ridiculous. That's like saying you can't prove that the President

lives in the White House by *looking into* the White House. It is looking into the White House that will provide the necessary proof. The fulfilled prophecies, the amazing consistency, and the many scientific statements of the Bible prove it to be the Word of God. They provide evidence that it is supernatural in origin.

8. While we do see variations within species—different types of dogs, etc. (*microevolution*)—we don't see any evidence of *macroevolution*—changes from one species to another. Microevolution is observable, while macroevolution takes a great leap of faith. If Christians had as much faith in God as atheists have in the theory of evolution, we would see revival. Like little children, evolutionists "believe" without a thread of observable evidence.

In 1980 about 150 of the world's leading evolutionary theorists gathered at the University of Chicago for a conference entitled "Macroevolution." Their task: "to consider the mechanisms that underlie the origin of species" (Lewin, *Science*, vol. 210, pp. 883–887). "The central question of the Chicago conference was whether the mechanisms underlying microevolution can be extrapolated to explain the phenomena of macroevolution...the answer can be given as a clear, No."

Thus the scientific observations support the creation tenet that each basic type is separate and distinct from all others, and that while variation is inevitable, macroevolution does not and did not happen.

9. "Did dinos soar? Imaginations certainly took flight over *Archaeoraptor Liaoningensis*, a birdlike fossil with a meat-eater's tail that was spirited out of northeastern China, 'discovered' at a Tucson, Arizona, gem and mineral show last year, and displayed at the National Geographic Society in Washington, D.C. Some 110,000 visitors saw the exhibit, which closed January 17; millions more read about the find in November's *National Geographic*. Now, paleontologists are eating crow. Instead of 'a true missing link' connecting dinosaurs to birds, the specimen appears to be a composite, its unusual appendage likely tacked on by a Chinese farmer, not evolution.

"*Archaeoraptor* is hardly the first 'missing link' to snap under scrutiny. In 1912, fossil remains of an ancient hominid were found in England's Piltdown quarries and quickly dubbed man's apelike ancestor. It took decades to reveal the hoax." *U.S. News & World Report*, February 14, 2000.

10. Quotes are from *The Expanded Quotable Einstein* (Princeton University Press).

11. I have found from experience that every argument of pseudo-intellectuals, who believe they are atheists, is about as impressive as a two-man "wave" at the Super Bowl. The arguments consistently reveal that they are either ignorant or deceived, by maintaining that the Bible says things that it doesn't. These arguments are looked at in-depth in *The Evidence Bible* (Bridge-Logos Publishers).

12. Other resources for learning how to share the gospel include *Hell's Best Kept Secret* (Whitaker House), *How to Win Souls and Influence People* (Bridge-Logos), and *Revival's Golden Key* (Bridge-Logos).

RESOURCES

Who Is the Lord of the Ring? The Gospel of John, uniquely formatted for those seeking the Supernatural. Discover why the ring's seal meant death to so many, and learn the identity of this Lord to whom even demons bow.

Scientific Facts in the Bible. Most people don't know that the Bible contains a wealth of scientific, medical, and prophetic facts. Gives compelling evidence that the Bible is no ordinary book.

Nostradamus: Attack on New York...and other Amazing Prophecies. Did Nostradamus predict the attack on the World Trade Center, Kennedy's assassination, and Hitler leading Germany? This book gives insight into the acclaimed prophecies of this famous prophet, and shows how he obtained his predictions.

The Evidence Bible. A comprehensive resource to help you share your faith and answer common objections to Christianity; offers hard evidence and scientific proof for the thinking mind. Commended by Josh McDowell, D. James Kennedy, and Franklin Graham. Finalist, 2002 Gold Medallion Book Award.

Revival's Golden Key. Learn how to share your faith biblically. "I have over 1,000 books on evangelism, soul-winning, and revival in my personal library and none of them are worthy to be compared to this book." —R. W. Jones, Word of Truth Ministries

Published by Bridge-Logos Publishers and
available through your local Christian bookstore

For a catalog of books, tracts, tapes, and videos by
Ray Comfort, visit our website at www.raycomfort.com,
call 800-437-1893, or write to: Living Waters Publications,
P. O. Box 1172, Bellflower, CA 90706.